PROVOCATIONS

STILL 'I FIND THAT OFFENSIVE!'

CLAIRE FOX

SERIES EDITOR:
YASMIN ALIBHAI-BROWN

Biteback Publishing

This new edition published in Great Britain in 2018 by
Biteback Publishing Ltd
Westminster Tower
3 Albert Embankment
London SE1 7SP
Copyright © Claire Fox 2016, 2018

ISBN 978-1-78590-416-5

10 9 8 7 6 5 4 3 2 1

A CIP catalogue record for this book is available from the British Library.

Set in Stempel Garamond by Adrian McLaughlin

Printed and bound in Great Britain by
CPI Group (UK) Ltd, Croydon CRO 4YY

MIX
Paper from
responsible sources
FSC® C020471

Contents

Dedication

I DEDICATE THIS BOOK to my much younger colleagues at the Academy of Ideas, who are an embodiment of the resilient and smart young people that are bold enough to want to change the world, however many insults are thrown at them. And also to the thousands of Debating Matters alumni, from sixth form to young adulthood, who are proof that arguing about ideas without restraint, learning to take criticism on the chin, having better things to do than feeling hurt, can help encourage others to be not so easily offended.

I offer special thanks to Rob Lyons, Austin Williams, David Bowden, Rossa Minogue and Geoff Kidder for reading first drafts and helping me to better articulate what I wanted to say.

Preface to the new edition

SINCE '*I Find That Offensive!*' was published, awareness of the campus free-speech wars has gone mainstream. Newspapers regularly feature the latest daft ban or lurid cultural appropriation story. Meanwhile 'Generation Snowflake', a term that *I Find This Offensive!* is credited with popularising in the UK (according to Wikipedia,[1] so it must be true) is also routinely deployed as a derogatory slap-down of any hint of thin-skinned offence-taking. The term has entered the Collins and Oxford dictionaries. *The Sun* newspaper even has a snowflake hotline. The government has also

---

1   Wikipedia definition of Generation Snowflake: https://en.wikipedia.org/wiki/Generation_Snowflake

intervened, supposedly on the side of free expression. In spring 2018, the government-backed campus free-speech summit[2] brought in tough new guidance that will discipline institutions if they allow 'valid debates to be shut down'. The new HE regulator, the Office for Students, has also been given powers to fine institutions for not upholding principles of free speech. So is all well? Are we witnessing a more liberal attitude to free expression?

Sadly not. Too often, as I warn in the book, campus free-speech controversies in particular are reduced to the extreme outliers, egregious examples easy to parody, but often missing the deeper problems. If we just focus on lurid (but true) tales of ludicrous trigger warnings or balaclava-wearing protesters closing down debates,[3] we avoid tackling more profound cultural

---

2   'Sam Gyimah hosts free speech summit', www.gov.uk, 3 May 2018: https://www.gov.uk/government/news/sam-gyimah-hosts-free-speech-summit

3   See for example the headline-grabbing campus scuffle involving Jacob Rees-Mogg at Bristol University (https://www.theguardian.com/politics/2018/feb/02/jacob-rees-mogg-involved-in-scuffle-at-university-campus) and the masked antifa invasion of a debate at King's College organised by the KCL Libertarian Society, which involved setting off smoke bombs and attacking security guards (http://www.dailymail.co.uk/news/article-5466359/Several-people-hurt-thugs-shut-FREE-SPEECH-event.html)

trends that normalise such censoriousness. What is more, the government's vow to stamp out the 'chilling' trend of blocking speakers from campuses might be well-meaning but risks tangling speech up in another layer of officially sanctioned regulation. It also adds fuel to a worrying new tendency: to deny that there is a free-speech crisis at all, simply writing off concerns as an exaggerated tabloid/Tory conspiracy, or the hubris of a bunch of grouchy baby boomers moaning about the new generation.

One of those who claims that campus censorship is exaggerated is Adam Tickell, vice-chancellor of the University of Sussex. He writes: 'Look closer and you will see that the evidence for [campus censorship] is vanishingly small.'[4] But it is Tickell who should take a closer look. A student society debate on free speech was recently banned at his own university.[5] One of his own colleagues, Dr Kathleen Stock, has been erroneously

4   Adam Tickell, 'Free-speech warriors mistake student protest for censorship', *The Guardian*, 7 May 2018

5   Jordan Wright, 'Union obliterates the debate – unwritten requirement used to shut down free speech debate', *The Badger*, 27 April 2018

defamed as 'transphobic' merely for writing an article for *The Economist* entitled 'Changing the concept
of "woman" will cause unintended harms', discussing
female interests in the transgender debate.[6] Denouncing her, the Sussex Students' Union Executive said, 'We
will not tolerate hate on our campus.'[7] Goldsmiths College has opened a speech-chilling 'hate crime reporting
centre'.[8] King's College now deploy sinister-sound-
ing safe space monitors to take 'immediate appropriate
action' if speech codes are breached.[9] Many universities demand pre-vetting of speeches for external college
speakers.[10] This insidious, often bureaucratic, chipping

---

6   Kathleen Stock, 'Changing the concept of "woman" will cause unintended
harms', *The Economist*, 6 July 2018

7   'Statement from University of Sussex Students' Union Exec', 9
July 2018: https://www.sussexstudent.com/news/article/ussu/
Statement-from-University-of-Sussex-Students-Union-Exec/

8   'Hate crime reporting centre set up at Goldsmiths', 16 October 2017: https://
www.gold.ac.uk/news/hate-crime-reporting-centre/

9   Eleanor Rose, 'King's College London deploys "Safe Space Marshals" to
ensure students "don't have their feelings hurt" at talks', *Evening Standard*,
27 October 2017

10 Peter Hitchens, 'Why I climbed on my soapbox after refusing to sign a university's "free speech" contract', *The Spectator*, 4 November 2017

away at the freedom to discuss openly may not hit the headlines, but takes its toll, creating a climate inhospitable to debate.

One new twist in the free-speech wars is language manipulation. A whole new lexicon of words and phrases, such as 'fake news', 'post-truth', 'virtue signalling' has sprung up to dismiss others' opinions as not worth engaging with. Literary critic Houman Barekat explains that the term 'gaslighting' – accusing someone who challenges your viewpoint of a malicious assault on your right to be believed – is 'a lazy but effective way of shutting down dissent and disagreement'. It is, he says, 'a psychologised, left-leaning upgrade on the familiar Donald Trump refrain of "Fake News!"'[11] Accusing a questioner of gaslighting delegitimises the question.

Linguistic discrediting has become especially pronounced in the wake of anti-establishment democratic decisions such as Brexit and the election of Donald Trump. Millions of voters have been demonised as

---

11 Houman Barekat, 'Calling people out for "gaslighting" is just a lazy but effective way of shutting down dissent', *The Spectator*, 14 June 2018

deplorables, low-information xenophobes, 'gammons',[12] populists etc. Populism itself has moved from being a political science category to the insult *de nos jours*, given an entirely negative meaning. But if you can't vote freely – without being classified as beyond the pale – what hope for *speaking* freely? Once such patholo-gised monikers are applied, it becomes all too easy to disregard anything said by those so labelled. This has contributed to a febrile culture war, with serious impli-cations for engaging civilly with those we disagree with.

I am aware that there is an irony in these language wars. Labelling someone a snowflake can also be another way of silencing people. In a *Guardian* article entitled '"Poor little snowflake" – the defining insult of 2016', the author noted that 'the term "snowflake" has been thrown around with abandon in the wake of Brexit and the US election, usually to express generic disdain for young people'.[13] Snowflakery is undoubtedly used as

---

12 Thomas Mackie, 'Middle-aged white Brexit supporters called "GAMMON" by "SNOWFLAKE" left-wing CORBYNITES', *Daily Express*, 15 May 2018

13 Rebecca Nicholson, '"Poor little snowflake" – the defining insult of 2016', *The Guardian*, 28 November 2016

a dismissive insult, a way of lampooning the most out-landish aspects of the easily offended culture without actually engaging with it. But this is not a *mea culpa*. The *Collins Dictionary* definition, 'young adults … viewed as being less resilient and more prone to taking offence than previous generations', still applies. It rather makes my point that in one survey, 74 per cent of respondents aged 16–24 complained that merely being called 'snowflakes' could have a negative effect on their mental health.[14]

More positively, it's refreshing that some are rebelling against the caricature. Time and again, when speaking at schools and universities about *'I Find That Offensive!'*, I've heard students from all political persuasions talk of their frustration at their own generation's retreat into the conformity of divisive identity bubbles. While I dreaded that my book might be seen as a middle-aged woman bemoaning 'the youth of today', it has been gratifying that the most enthusiastic response has come from

---

14 'Don't call us snowflakes', Aviva press release, 6 December 2017: https://www.aviva.com/newsroom/news-releases/2017/12/dont_call_us_snowflakes/

under-25s, keen to break from endless restrictions on speaking and thinking freely. Most hostility has come from my own peers.

This is how it should be. I wasn't actually critiquing today's youth so much as that new class of educational and social policy 'experts', whose resilience-draining ideology is doing such a tragic disservice to younger generations. This trend is intensifying. Just look at the so-called epidemic of youth mental ill-health, which all too often leads to an infantilised view of young adults. It is no coincidence that Sam Gyimah, Minister for Higher Education, cited the student mental health crisis as a reason for university authorities to act *in loco parentis*.[15] Even NUS head of policy and campaigns David Malcolm spotted the danger of expanding the duty of care far beyond the academic aspects of university life. He noted that it could lead to a return to 'the paternalism of the 1950s and 1960s' and warned against invoking 'the spirit of an age when students were very much treated

---

15 'Student Mental Health – New package of measures announced', London School of Business and Management, 2 July 2018: https://www.lsbm.ac.uk/headline/news_detail/244

like … children' with its 'curfews and prohibitions on overnight guests'.[16]

Ironically, one reason students are viewed (indeed view themselves) as psychologically vulnerable and in need of third-party intervention is NUS-led campaigns that emphasise the so-called anxiety-inducing perils of modern campus life and promote a model of fragile undergraduates in need of support (see pp. 137–8). So it's no surprise when their adult autonomy is challenged by politicians. And despite those same politicians talking the free-speech talk, they fail to grasp that the roots of censoriousness lie in over-coddling, as my book argues. The tendency for young people to view themselves as uniquely in need of protection from psychological harm – including ideas that unsettle – partly explains why they seem prone to regard unfettered speech as an existential threat.

This institutional tendency to medicalise young people's experience continues to have a counter-productive effect, intensifying a sense that students are unable to cope.

---

16 David Malcolm, '"As much freedom as is good for them" – looking back at in loco parentis', wonkhe.com, 7 March 2018: https://wonkhe.com/blogs/much-freedom-good-looking-back-loco-parentis/

Minding Our Future, a recent report by Universities UK, reveals that the number of students dropping out with mental health problems has more than trebled in recent years.[17] Even political challenges are categorised as therapeutic problems. In July 2017, one survey asked 4,000 16–30-year-olds about their anxieties; one of the most commonly cited (42 per cent) was leaving the European Union.[18] The Mental Health Foundation even has a 'Coping with post Brexit anxiety' page on its website.[19] Yet a common reaction to my book has been for professional youth spokespeople and their cheerleaders to repackage such psychologising of political disputes as proof of how politically sensitive and caring today's young are.[20]

Natasha Devon, formerly the government's mental

---

17 *Minding Our Future*, Universities UK, 11 May 2018: https://www.universitiesuk.ac.uk/policy-and-analysis/reports/Documents/2018/minding-our-future-starting-conversation-student-mental-health.pdf

18 The Young Women's Trust annual report, tellingly entitled *Worrying Times*. See Phillip Inman, 'Young people "more anxious than ever" due to Brexit and rising debt', *The Guardian*, 29 September 2017

19 https://www.mentalhealth.org.uk/blog/coping-post-brexit-anxiety

20 Richard Brooks, 'In defence of generation snowflake – everyone's favourite punching bag', *Daily Telegraph*, 14 November 2016

health tsar, commends the 'bravery required to call out attitudes one finds distasteful', stating that 'it doesn't threaten free speech – it broadens debate'.[21] But no amount of flattery can disguise the fact that the recent history of calling out distasteful attitudes (by branding opponents as misogynist, transphobes, racists) is actually closing down debate and betraying real justice; for minorities, for the young, for all of us.

Worryingly, this call-out culture has now turned its sights on delegitimising the very fight for free speech and demonising its advocates. It is now commonplace for radicals, such as Owen Jones, to dismiss those fighting censorious trends as 'rightwing, well-heeled, white, straight male ... bigots who clothe themselves in the garb of free speech [but] have no real interest in it. They just want the right to hate without challenge.'[22] Quite an accusation! However, it fits a broader pattern of impugning the motives of free-speech activists.

---

21 Natasha Devon, 'Young people's passion for a fairer world should be embraced, not ridiculed', *The Guardian*, 13 June 2016

22 Owen Jones, 'Giving the "gay cure" quack a TV platform is an abuse of free speech', *The Guardian*, 7 September 2017

As a result, *Guardian* columnist Nesrine Malik can claim that 'freedom of speech is no longer a value. It has become a loophole exploited with impunity by trolls, racists and ethnic cleansing advocates.'[23] Those who cannot so easily be dismissed as bigots – anti-racist or civil libertarian liberals, perhaps – are dismissed as the useful idiots 'free-speech grifters' who rail against 'PC culture as the main threat to the freedom of expression' and are therefore condemned for unwittingly playing the right's game. A similar point is made in the publicity for Yasmin Alibhai-Brown's new book *In Defence of Political Correctness*. She worries that 'intolerance is justified through [the] invocation of liberty', describing a dystopian world in which 'anti-political correctness has gone mad'. These commentators are so appalled by dodgy right-wingers' association with free speech, by the likes of outrage-monger Milo Yiannopoulos or shock-jock Katie Hopkins styling themselves as free-speech martyrs, that they are prepared to throw the baby out with the bathwater to

---

23 Nesrine Malik, 'Hate speech leads to violence. Why would liberals defend it?', *The Guardian*, 22 March 2018

avoid contamination by association.[24] Once liberal principles can be ditched as tainted by dint of being espoused by those you despise, a cowardly retreat from defending free-speech wars' casualties ensues. Two tales illustrate the real cost of this prevarication.

A tale of two women
Tale 1: The wrong sort of minority

On 6 May 2018, a sunny Bank Holiday Sunday, well-known drag queen Vanity von Glow performed at a London demonstration labelled 'Day of Freedom'. Within hours, Vanity (real name Thom Glow), found herself at the centre of a Twitter storm that seemed designed to destroy her career. A lifelong Labour supporter, Vanity was damned for sharing a platform with other speakers dubbed 'far-right' by various media commentators[25]

---

24 Simon Childs, 'What the Far-Right Mean When They Say "Free Speech"', *Vice*, 9 May 2018

25 See, as a typical example of the rally's write-up in the broadsheets, Ellie Mae O'Hagan, 'The far right is rising, and Britain is dangerously complacent about it', *The Guardian*, 7 May 2018

(although some would dispute this, and one commentator notes how the label is used too promiscuously these days, often as a way of undermining free speech activism).[26] It was guilt by association.

It's true that the 'Day for Freedom' was dominated by figures from the right (the rally was called following a Twitter ban of former EDL leader Tommy Robinson). However, as stand-up comedian Andrew Doyle points out, this may be 'largely a symptom of the left's growing hostility towards the principle of free expression'.[27] That Vanity attended is perhaps to her credit. She explained afterwards that she accepted the request to appear because she felt she 'would be a hypocrite to only champion free speech when it suits my own ideological ends'. Regardless, her views were conflated with the organisers'.

A ferocious backlash led to her losing bookings at a

---

26 One free speech activist notes: 'Prominent left-wing voices have continually sought to broaden the scope of terms such as "far right" and "alt-right" to incorporate as many of their ideological opponents as possible.' See Andrew Doyle, 'The Day for Freedom was not a far-right rally', spiked, 9 May 2018

27 Andrew Doyle, 'Vanity Von Glow: The left eats its own', spiked, 6 June 2018

variety of clubs at which she was due to appear. Vanity – a regular act at LGBT+ venues, who performed on the main stage at London Pride in 2017 – was barred, banned, ostracised. Queer cabaret bar Her Upstairs cancelled her performance because the rally 'organisers stand for fundamental values that directly contradict what we believe in'. In its judgemental statement it declared: 'Whilst like everyone she has the right to freedom of speech, her alignment with such an event calls into question her motives ... She will no longer be booked at Her Upstairs.'[28] The Phoenix Artist Club cancelled her appearance at 'A Night in Soho', illustrating how once you have established a 'guilt-by-association' precedent, it becomes a roller-coaster: 'We are furious about any suggested association that has been made between our club and the right-wing speakers at this rally and we think Vanity in time will regret her decision,'[29] they chided.

---

28 Posted on Her Upstairs Facebook page on 7 May 2018: https://www.facebook.com/HerUpstairsLondon/posts/1121914874615780

29 Mimi Launder, 'London drag queen Vanity von Glow performed at a far-right rally and now she's losing bookings', indy100, 8 May 2018

In fact, Vanity's response has been commendably consistent, which draws our attention to the dangerous hypocrisy of the 'hang 'er out to dry' brigade. Interviewed on Sky News, Vanity noted that for years the far right had insulted her as perverted, whereas today the left are 'just as bad': 'They're not just calling me a degenerate, they're also calling me a fascist.' Her complaint was not just the demonisation:

> The far left don't just go for calling you names. Their party trick at the moment is to … go for your source of income. They've been making sure that my shows are cancelled. They want to see me unemployed … It's quite an aggressive tactic simply for disagreeing with my motives for attending an event.[30]

Why did the usual suspect campaigners for social justice fail to support LGBT+ activist Von Glow (a seasoned performer but only twenty-nine years old) after what

---

30 Jess Glass, 'Drag queen Vanity von Glow blames the "far left" for damaging her career after appearing at "far right" rally', Pink News, 11 May 2018

amounted to a political boycott? It seems that there are certain causes that are worthy of support, and others that can be dismissed because they might endorse the 'wrong' message. *The Guardian*'s Malik is one of increasing numbers to push the idea that 'the right to a platform isn't absolute', preferring a narrow legalistic understanding of censorship: 'If you are not being convicted and penalised by the state for speaking, then you have freedom of speech.'

Despite endless examples of devastating, reputation-shaming consequences of non-state call-outs for saying the 'wrong' thing in public and private, Sam Leith is equally complacent in arguing that the fight for free speech should be 'against state censorship and the imprisonment of writers ... and intimidation by quasi-statal institutions'. What about the quasi-censorship and intimidation of a drag queen? Sam thinks that all that happens to those who 'say something offensive' (who of course he whimsically assumes will be those who 'turn up at a costume party blacked up or dressed as a Wehrmacht officer') is that 'you can expect to cop some flak ... you may well suffer an influx of angry eggs. But you won't go to jail.'[31] My next tale demonstrates how such blasé attitudes and blind eyes mean that there are creeping criminal law interventions into freedom of speech, with minimal opposition.

Tale 2: The wrong sort of youths

In April 2018, a court found nineteen-year-old Chelsea Russell from Liverpool guilty of sending a 'grossly offensive' message. Her sentence was increased from a fine to an eight-week community order when it was deemed a 'hate crime'.[32] She was placed on an eight-week curfew from 8 p.m. to 8 a.m., fitted with an electronic ankle bracelet and told to pay £500 costs and an £85 victim surcharge.

Her 'crime'? She had posted the lyrics from American rapper Snap Dogg's 'I'm Trippin", to pay tribute to thirteen-year-old Frankie Murphy, who died after he was

---

31 Sam Leith, 'Conservatives are wrong about free speech', *The Spectator*, 7 July 2018

32 Tom Duffy, 'Woman who posted rap lyrics as tribute on Instagram guilty of sending offensive message', *Liverpool Echo*, 17 April 2018

hit by a car in 2017. She was charged after a screenshot of her Instagram post, quoting the lyrics 'kill a snitch n***a and rob a rich n***a', was anonymously sent to Merseyside Police's Constable Dominique Walker, based within a specialist police hate crime unit. PC Walker seemed to take personal offence. She told the court the term n***a was 'grossly offensive' to her as a black woman and to the general community. She even asked the defence lawyer not to use the word in court. Russell's defence argued – among other things – that the word had been used by superstar rapper Jay-Z 'in front of thousands of people at the Glastonbury Festival' and cited the Urban Dictionary, which said that the word ending in the letter 'a' meant a 'black man wearing a gold chain'. To no avail. District Judge Jack McGarva said, 'There is no place in civil society for language like that. Everyone with an Instagram account could view this content. The lyrics also encourage killing and robbing, so are grossly offensive.'

So a young woman now has a criminal record – she is a hate criminal – for copying lyrics that the police and courts find offensive. No broadsheet headlines. No campaigns against state censorship. Forty years ago, attempting to prosecute *Never Mind the Bollocks* for breaching Victorian indecency standards was thought to be absurd and the case was thrown out. Not so today, apparently.

Such criminalisation has become so routine that there is a law on the statute books[33] which sees nine people arrested every day in the UK for their online posts.[34] All you have to say is something 'deemed to be' hateful or grossly offensive and social justice campaigners look the other way. We are led to believe that the victims of such hate crimes are the oppressed, right? In this instance, the main offended victim seems to have been a police officer – but she is black and a woman, so perhaps in the weird hierarchy of intersectional identity politics that makes her a victim – an object of sympathy – rather than someone with the authority to criminalise a rap-loving Scouser.

Ms Russell was possibly lucky to have been sentenced in 2018, as punishments for such crimes look likely to get

---

33 Specifically, Section 127 of the Communications Act 2003: https://www.legislation.gov.uk/ukpga/2003/21/section/127

34 Charlie Parker, 'Police arresting nine people a day in fight against hate trolls', *The Times*, 12 October 2017

scarier in the future. The Sentencing Council for England and Wales has declared that the use of social media, YouTube, and other websites to 'stir hatred' is a growing problem, and is proposing far harsher sentences for anyone perceived as targeting online 'protected characteristics' including 'race; sex; disability; age; sexual orientation; religion or belief; pregnancy and maternity; and gender reassignment'. Anyone who is queasy about the Gender Recognition Act, those who are regularly labelled transphobic TERFs by trans activists – BEWARE what you tweet. No evidence is needed to bring a criminal complaint. Hate speech trolling, which includes everything from retweets to commenting on others' posts, could face between six months and six years in jail.

This follows recent CPS guidelines that expand hate policing online to 'any criminal offence which is *perceived* by the victim or any other person, to be motivated by a hostility or prejudice' (my emphasis).[35] We should expect to see worse punishments than that meted out

---

35 Alison Saunders, 'Hate is hate. Online abusers must be dealt with harshly', *The Guardian*, 21 August 2017

to Ms Russell when thin-skinned 'victims' start claiming that they are offended by what they've read online.

Meanwhile, another cohort of young people are having their civil rights taken from them, with little or no comment from the selectively outraged. This time it is mainly black teenagers affected, and once again hateful lyrics are in the frame. In wake of the rise in violent gang crime in London, Metropolitan Police Commissioner Cressida Dick has demanded that music lyrics and online videos that glamorise violence should be banned.[36] She wasn't referring to 'I Shot the Sheriff', of course, but singled out 'drill music' (a style of rap music originated in Chicago). YouTube has obliged, removing thirty videos to date.[37] Now London's 1011 drill group has been issued with a court order banning them from recording or performing music without permission from Scotland Yard, a legal first in the UK.[38]

---

36 Andrew Trendell, 'YouTube deletes half of "violent" music videos, with police singling out "drill music"', NME, 29 May 2018

37 See also 'Police to treat gangs like terror suspects with tough new laws', *Daily Telegraph*, 30 May 2018

38 El Hunt, 'Drill group banned from making music without police permission', NME, 15 June 2018

Drill artists, Ms Russell and teenage trolls might be unlikely free-speech causes célèbres but, unlike campus radicals or social justice keyboard warriors, they have no safe spaces to hide in, and precious few allies among their radical peers, despite being the target of draconian laws and grave injustice. My message to those indignant that Generation Snowflake is a myth: prove it. Show your free-speech credentials – join the fight for Vanity von Glow. Support the Liverpool 1. For those already convinced that we need a new free-speech movement, turn off those Jordan Peterson YouTube videos long enough to take on the hard cases. Consistency is the key. Defend EVERYONE'S free speech and be aware of the real enemies: those who seek to delegitimise free speech; those who preach that censorship is overstated, that there's 'nothing to see here'. That's only because they haven't opened their eyes.

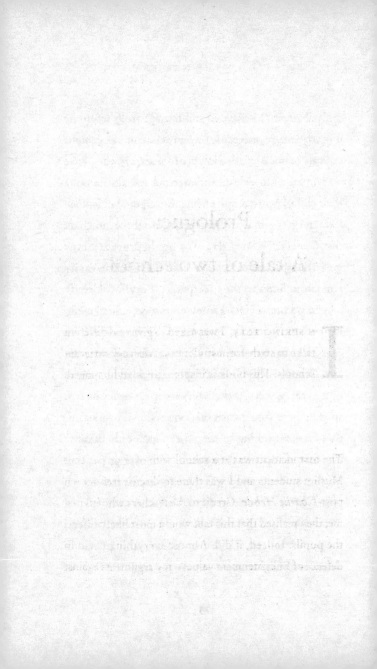

Prologue:
A tale of two schools

I N SPRING 2015, I was asked to give two different talks to sixth-form students at two very different schools. This book is inspired by what happened.

*   *   *

The first incident was at a school with over 90 per cent Muslim students and I was there to discuss free speech post-*Charlie Hebdo*. Credit to the teachers who invited me; they realised that this talk would most likely offend the pupils. Indeed, it did. Almost everything I said in defence of Enlightenment values – my arguments against protecting any one group, whether based on religion, ethnicity or sexuality, from offence – was met with gasps of disbelief. At one point I apparently made a religious *faux pas* when I explained, 'It doesn't matter how upset people were by a picture of Mohammed on a magazine front cover, the point is...' and was interrupted by screeches of horror. I had seemingly broken some rule by failing to say '*The Prophet* Mohammed'. While a minority heckled 'how dare you', many seemed more upset than angry. Some of the girls in the front row looked close to tears. I feared that some were ready to walk out and I had to shout through the uproar, explaining that I was there to talk about free speech, not theology. While I had not sought to be gratuitously offensive about Mohammed, I urged them to listen to my arguments and discuss with me, rather than being outraged about a linguistic mistake. It took a while before relative calm was restored, but what struck me was how distressed they were by my remarks. This was not a feigned response or an affectation; they had been genuinely hurt.

In the discussion that followed, it became clear that these lovely, bright young people had found it difficult to hear my arguments without taking them personally. The girls in particular seemed distraught, as though I had insulted each one of them rather than making a general case for free speech. One young woman, her voice quivering, explained that she felt devastated whenever the Prophet Mohammed was disrespected. Another tearfully said that maybe non-Muslims didn't care about the precise use of words or images but, for her, seeing something like the *Hebdo* cartoons was, she explained, like being physically assaulted or being exposed to the vilest pornography. And while some of this may have been a demonstration of typical teenage melodrama, the pupils did seem taken aback that I was prepared to stand up to their diktats – telling me what I was permitted to say about *their* religion – without being defensive about challenging some of their ill-informed prejudices. When I took on one boy's conspiracy theory that there was no proof that Islamic terrorists had perpetrated 9/11, he replied, 'Well that's just your opinion.' Other pupils argued against him, but suggested I needed to make allowances. Several London-born-and-raised teenagers explained that maybe, as a Western woman, I needed to be more sensitive; I couldn't possibly understand their pain or the suffering of the worldwide Ummah. Maybe, one pupil suggested, I should listen to him, not the other way round.

As many more tried to inform me that Europe was awash with Islamophobia, I managed to challenge them, but found it difficult to reassure these genuinely frightened pupils with facts. They quoted mainstream politicians and news programmes on the dangers of a backlash post-*Charlie Hebdo*, and seemed to believe that anything less than uncritical respect for Islam amounted to hate speech and was just one step away from anti-Muslim pogroms.

I got through the event shaken but intrigued. The hard-pressed teachers seemed delighted that I had started a debate. When I related this story afterwards, many people concluded that the problem here was the nature of Islam. They suggested that the Koran, or a perverted reading of it, had somehow taught these pupils intolerance and had bred a particular inability to have their views challenged. But, actually, the reception to my remarks was personal, and I recognised that look of hurt in the pupils' eyes when I criticised their views. I had seen a similar thin-skinned reaction before: when I received an almost identical response from a completely different group of pupils to a speech on a completely different topic.

At the second school, I had been asked to debate the motion 'Ched Evans: social justice or mob rule?', about whether footballer Ched Evans, a released convicted rapist, should ever be employed to play professional football again. I was on the back foot from the start. The allegedly neutral sixth-former introducing the debate explained that, as a feminist, she was against rehabilitating rapists. My official opponent, a well-known TV personality, followed on with a rousing speech about the horrors of rape. When she asked 25 per cent of the audience to stand up so that she could illustrate how many of them were likely to end up being sexually assaulted, the pupils were gripped. That infamous 'one in four' stat may be inaccurate, but it has become an unchallengeable truth. My rather dry defence of rehabilitation, the rule of law, natural justice, impartiality, a fresh start once you have done your time, and the dangers of emotionally clouded judgements on sentencing were never likely to win me allies. They didn't.

But it was when the Q&A started that things really heated up. It became obvious that there was an accepted, acceptable narrative here, and any challenge to it led to accusations of victim-blaming or rape apologism. The contributions became increasingly shrill, with several students demanding that anyone convicted of rape should be locked up for life and denied the right to be a father, let alone be allowed to have a job. It was then that it dawned on me that one of the reasons that my arguments were making little headway was that the students had already internalised the 'fact' that rape and sexual assault were unquestionably the most heinous thing that could ever happen, a crime beyond forgiveness, and that its victims would never be able to get over it. Whatever I said was secondary. The definitions of rape being used by the pupils were very broad, incorporating everything from unwanted advances to regretted sex, and were being discussed as though it was an imminent threat to each and every one of them.

I was genuinely worried that these students – particularly the young women – would fare badly in the post-school real world if they were so terrified. I decided, perhaps rashly (quoting Germaine Greer for recognisable feminist cred), to tell them that rape was not necessarily the worst thing that could ever happen to an individual. Yes, it is a serious crime, but we need a sense of proportion. The room erupted. The audience shrieked. A teacher yelled out, 'You can't say that.' Girls were hugging each other for comfort. The majority seemed shell-shocked. Even *posing* this viewpoint was a step too far, it seemed. I was told that I was dangerous, irresponsible and offensive. My careless comments, they told me, could send a message to the young men present that sexual assault was OK.

As in the first school, pupils' reactions betrayed a genuinely felt personal hurt and surprise that I – or anyone – could say the unsayable out loud and then refuse to back off when they told me, 'You can't say that.' One pupil came up to me, not to shake my hand, but to tell me that my views had made her feel nauseous. A group of emotional girls suggested that maybe as an older woman I needed to be more sensitive to the plight of younger women and that I obviously had no empathy with women worldwide who are raped daily.

I am pretty hard-nosed, and I don't take pleasure in making teenagers cry, but these reactions did shake me up. What these two schools had in common were teenagers who believed that words really hurt and that contradictory opinions to their own beliefs were the cause of real harm.

And yet, despite the pupils' apparent hyper-sensitivity, their emotional suffering was combined with an almost belligerent sense of entitlement that their feelings should take precedence. In both instances, I was put under pressure to retract, apologise and assuage students' distress. While these young Muslims and young feminists may superficially seem to have little in common, they were indistinguishable from each other in demanding bans and apologies for what they considered offensive, dangerous ideas. Both groups agreed that my advice that 'sticks and stones might break your bones, but words will never hurt me' was an outdated misunderstanding of the fundamental damage that words can inflict on vulnerable individuals.

My tale of two schools captures trends that I have been worrying about for some time. At school or university events, I have noticed an increasingly prickly willingness to take offence – and the corrosive effect that this is having on attitudes to free speech. This trend, to be easily offended, is now exploding into public consciousness with the unravelling madness that has taken over so many American universities, and is now emerging on British campuses. Spiked's Free Speech University Rankings 2018[39] show that 94 per cent of universities and students' unions censor speech. Rising from 80 per cent in 2015, the vast majority of these censorious policies are carried out by students' unions. Barely a week goes by without reports of something 'offensive' being banned from campus. But dubbing students as cry-babies and 'snowflakes' for their thin-skinned reactions to everything from Halloween costumes to song lyrics, statues to tabloid newspapers, doesn't really explain *why* this is happening.

Should we worry about such silly, trivial incidents? Perhaps we can just wait for these fragile youths to

---

39 Free Speech University Rankings, spiked, April 2018

grow up and not worry too much about broader consequences for society. However, this all-pervading sense of grievance, displayed by so many students, is now beginning to cause serious anguish for older commentators, who look on with horror at the increasing evidence that young people have become dangerously thin-skinned. This reflects worries that the young are becoming too mollycoddled and infantilised for the rough and tumble of real life.

When Dr Everett Piper, president of Oklahoma Wesleyan University, issued an open letter to his students saying 'This is not a day care. This is a university,' he was quoted internationally because he captured concerns about a generation who too often behave more like sulky, demanding children than young adults. Others are exasperated with the petty nature of contemporary complaints that seem so po-faced, joyless and censorious. Comedians such as Jerry Seinfeld, Chris Rock and Bill Maher have publicly condemned the oversensitivity of college students, saying too many of them can't take a joke. Even President Obama has weighed in during an interview with National Public Radio in December 2015, in which he told students that they should engage in debate with those who share different beliefs: 'Feel free to disagree with somebody, but don't try to just shut them up.' And in her first interview as new vice-chancellor of Oxford University, Professor Louise Richardson (the first female VC in the university's history) raised concerns about free speech on campus, explaining why it is positive for students to be exposed to 'uncomfortable' and 'objectionable' ideas.

Theme and structure of this book

It's hard not to become irritated about the younger generation when we hear that delegates at NUS Women's Conference find applause to be so stressful that they announced: 'Some delegates are requesting that we move to jazz hands rather than clapping, as it's triggering anxiety.' When a student union bans sombreros as offensive to Mexicans, or another condemns a yoga club for 'cultural appropriation', the young can seem exasperating. But, while there are plenty of easy targets to snigger at, it is much harder to work out who and what is responsible for what US public intellectual Todd Gitlin describes as a new 'generational norm of fragility'.

So this short book will explore why the young, in particular, have developed this insidious deference to offence. I will not deal with the main explanation, which is undoubtedly the decline of a liberal commitment to free speech. (For a full account, see Mick Hume's book *Trigger Warning: Is the Fear of Being Offensive Killing Free Speech?*) More modestly, I want to concentrate on identifying a number of problematic cultural and educational culprits that have softened up today's young, making them susceptible to easy offence. You see, young people are the expression of a problem that is actually caused by the retreat from reason by the older generation. We can sneer at youth's foolishness, but we need to take a long, hard look at official social policy influences that have created this generation out of the raw material of the previous one.

Part I surveys the contemporary offence scene, using examples from Britain and America. (Events in the US are often a useful warning of what is to come here.) It looks at the new trends on and off campus that are threatening free speech, from the privileging of victimhood and the splintering of identity to the new theories of microaggressions and the toxicity of Twitter.

Part II looks at therapeutic educational interventions, such as anti-bullying campaigns, through which the young are taught that psychological harm is interchangeable with physical violence, and which emphasise that safety is a virtue that trumps all else. This part also explores the industries that promote and encourage narcissistic tendencies in the young, from self-esteem to student voice.

Part III is a call to arms to the young, and a sketch of the challenges they face.

Before I start, I want to introduce a rider: I write this knowing that not all Millennials, Gen Y, Gen Z, NetGen, iGen etc. are spoilt wimps or over-anxious cry-babies. So if you count yourself among these groups, don't take it personally when I describe generational trends that are less than flattering. I feel for Joshi Herrmann, executive editor of *The Tab*, when he pleads, 'It would be cool if everyone could stop treating the authoritarian streak of a small minority of activists as a generational bellwether.'[40] But we need to confront these trends head-on, precisely to arm Joshi and his pro-free-speech peers with the intellectual arguments needed to create a new *zeitgeist*. So, let's start with a survey of the contemporary offence landscape.

40 Joshi Herrmann, 'Now the NUS is making our whole generation look bad', *The Tab*, 14 February 2016

Part I

'You can't say that' – walking on eggshells

I find that offensive

WHEN YOU HEAR that now ubiquitous but dread phrase, 'I find that offensive', you know you're being told to shut up. It is a commonplace way of ensuring that we are all self-conscious about what we say out loud, who and what we criticise, and guarantees we pull our punches in public debates, on social media, in workplaces, even in private exchanges. And the consequences of not heeding its moral stricture can be severe. The terrible murder of *Charlie Hebdo*'s staff in January 2015 demonstrated that those who offend can face the most brutal form of censorship.

After the massacre, which has become the iconic free-speech issue of recent times, there was some brief hope that this awful event might be enough to make people sit up and realise the importance of the right to be offensive. On Twitter, #JeSuisCharlie briefly flickered as one of the most widely used hashtags in history; it seemed to represent a universal cry of support for free expression. This defiance was tragically short-lived. Before long, 'Je Ne Suis Pas Charlie' became fashionable among growing numbers who declared the inflammatory nature of the offensive cartoons were at least indirectly responsible for triggering the slaughter.

This accommodation to offence is in no small part because, in the years before the *Charlie Hebdo* attack, there already existed a threatening, if not violent, climate that dictated that we all have to walk on eggshells and think twice before speaking up to avoid saying anything someone else might deem offensive. Since the attack, if anything, this atmosphere has only intensified.

To set the scene, let's look at some recent 'offence'

controversies and what they tell us about today's thin-skinned culture. Many of these point to the themes in Part Two, but also raise additional worrying consequences of an offence-seeking society.

It's not just students, stupid

When I started writing this book, I was concerned that UK readers would not be familiar with terms such as 'safe spaces', 'microaggressions' and 'trigger warnings'. Perhaps these were once confined to the outer margins of US university madness, but things have moved on. These trends are now not only features of UK university life, but events are unravelling so rapidly that such ideas are seeping out from campus into the mainstream. Similarly, some of my political peers have been rather disdainful about the importance I place on highlighting university offence disputes, suggesting these are atypical, the preserve of a small minority, immature skirmishes with little impact on the real world. However, this is to underestimate the trend and misunderstand how what happens on campus is a grotesque mirror of a broader cultural climate of censoriousness. In reality, all sorts of people feel one offensive comment away from someone else's outraged hashtag campaign. The language of offence is now part and parcel of popular culture. A contestant is as likely to get kicked out of the *Big Brother* house for allegedly homophobic or racist comments as they are from any university campus. Since Jade Goody's eviction in 2007 for making remarks deemed to be racist,[41] policing language for offence has been a core feature of the show's diary-room reprimands.

At the other end of the cultural spectrum, but just as mainstream, the arts world is increasingly affected by offence controversies. When the Barbican was forced to close *Exhibit B* in September 2014 due to protests over its recreation of a colonial-era 'human zoo', just a month after protesters closed an Israeli hip-hop show at the Edinburgh Festival Fringe, there was understandable concern about the emergence of a new 'heckler's veto'. Now there are fears of self-censorship as well. For example, Amsterdam's renowned art

---

41 'I'm not racist, says TV's Goody', BBC News, 20 January 2007

gallery the Rijksmuseum has announced it is to change the 'offensive' titles in its collection, replacing any references to Mohammedan, Negro, Indian, dwarf and Eskimo with PC-friendly terminology. Thus Simon Maris's *Young Negro Girl* (c. 1900) has become *Young Girl Holding a Fan*.

The offence wars are not outlier incidents confined to the margins of academia or PC madness. It is worth noting that the first big politics story of 2016 saw demands that David Cameron's policy chief, Oliver Letwin MP, apologise over 'offensive' remarks he made thirty years ago about blaming the black community's 'bad morals' for the Broadwater Farm riots. He duly apologised. Next?

The big sports story to start the year focused on outrage over Jamaican cricketer Chris Gayle asking sports journalist Mel McLaughlin out for a drink during a TV interview: 'Hopefully we can win this game and we can have a drink afterwards. Don't blush, baby.' His remarks were denounced as 'completely inappropriate and disrespectful', a form of sexual harassment. Gayle was given a fine of AU$10,000. Next?

One of the first parliamentary debates of 2016 was a three-hour session in response to a 570,000-signature petition to ban US presidential candidate Donald Trump from Britain, following his offensive demand for a 'total and complete shutdown' of Muslims entering the US. With no sense of irony, the petition made a virtue of the fact that the UK itself has a fine track record of shutting down entry to its shores: 'The Home Secretary has explicitly excluded eighty-four people for hate speech. My view is that Donald Trump should be number eighty-five.' As these eighty-four were banned for their dangerous ideas, that seemed OK with activists. Next...?

These examples are just three that hit the headlines in the UK in 2016 and all before the third week of January. The more interminable offence skirmishes take place away from the spotlight but are now a regular feature of many people's everyday interactions at work, on social media, in the public and private sphere. It can seem exhausting to always have to watch what you say, knowing that once you let your guard down you could be 'called out' for offending someone. This has created a febrile atmosphere that encourages people to disengage from debate to avoid the heat. A writer and self-styled 'socially liberal critic of today's social liberalism', Fredrik deBoer sums up the mood of retreat:

> There are so many ways to step on a land mine now, so many terms that have become forbidden, so many attitudes that will get you cast out if you even appear to hold them. I'm far from alone in feeling that it's typically not worth it to engage, given the risks.[42]

Not the usual suspects

This escalating offence-spotting is unnerving, especially when you realise that the target list for people likely to be hauled over the coals for being offensive is growing. Anyone can be accused, and the most liberal organisations can crumble when under fire. In 2013, *The Observer* published feminist Julie Burchill's defence of

---

42 Fredrik deBoer, 'Where Online Social Liberalism Lost The Script', The Dish, 21 August 2014

fellow *Guardian* writer Suzanne Moore after Moore had been criticised for transphobia for what she wrote in an article in the *New Statesman*. Burchill found that she, too, was monstered. Most significantly, after complaints by other feminists, Burchill's opinion piece, railing against a 'bunch of dicks in chicks' clothing', was promptly removed from the website of one of Britain's most liberal newspapers for containing too many offensive opinions.

There is a similar tale of 'not the usual suspects' at universities. Inevitably, most of the targets are the predictable *bêtes noires* of left/feminist-leaning students, with bans and offence *fatwas* issued against: *The Sun*, because Page Three 'normalises rape'; comedian Dapper Laughs, for being too laddish; columnist Katie Hopkins, the self-proclaimed 'slayer of PC'; Breitbart controversialist and men's rights supporter Milo Yiannopoulos. Yet, today, you don't have to be schlock jock or reactionary to be pilloried for the wrong opinions; just being the wrong sort of feminist is enough. Examples are multiplying, such as attempts in 2015 to ban such iconic figures as Germaine Greer and renowned ex-Muslim secular campaigner Maryam Namazie from speaking at various universities.[43] Debating free speech is itself now targeted. Gay-rights campaigner Peter Tatchell and classics scholar Mary Beard, who both signed a letter in *The Observer* defending academic freedom, were bombarded by hate tweets and a campaign of vilification. Indeed, Fran Cowling, the NUS's LGBT representative, recently refused to share a platform with Tatchell at Canterbury Christ Church University due to this very letter, branding him 'racist' and 'transphobic'.[44] Anti-domestic violence campaigner and feminist activist Julie Bindel, who has been repeatedly no-platformed as 'vile' and transphobic (because of a 2004 *Guardian* article that few have read but which has entered into folklore), was disinvited by Manchester University's Students' Union from a debate about – wait for it – free speech and feminism.

Then there was the 2015 offence row centring on sassy

43 Helen Lewis, 'What the row over banning Germaine Greer is really about', *New Statesman*, 27 October 2015

44 Rob Waugh, 'Gay activist Peter Tatchell is branded "transphobic" by NUS representative', *Metro*, 15 February 2016

female rock star Chrissie Hynde. Despite the Pretenders singer being a hard-rocking trailblazer, who proved women could match their male peers in a man's world, she still managed to fall foul of the offence brigade for, of all things, betraying women. Hynde gave an interview in which she admitted that she now regretted doing some stupid, reckless things in her past, including one that ended in a horrible sexual assault: 'Possibly getting off your face and getting out of it, hanging out with motorcycle gangs and being lairy is inadvisable.' Her mistake was being honest enough to admit some culpability. Social media exploded and a victim, speaking out about her own abuse, was publicly shamed for being offensive and, to add insult to injury, accused of victim-shaming. While anti-rape campaigners are constantly telling women they should speak out about their experiences, in this instance, where someone did, she was howled down by a self-selected group of feminist 'experts' for not sending out 'the right message'.

This problem is not about one person as such, or confined to one issue. This climate of censoriousness effectively locks down opinions, dictating that there can be no debate off script about certain issues. This has a chilling effect on everyone. Regardless of whether you agree with Hynde, her views seem a reasonable basis for an interesting and important discussion about whether absolving women of all responsibility for their actions is liberating or demeaning. Bandying around the phrase 'rape apologist' can only have the effect of silencing anyone who doesn't just parrot the current, prescriptive, feminist orthodoxy. And if a female icon can be hounded for speaking out of turn, imagine what would happen to any man sharing such a viewpoint.

Even asking questions is banned in this climate. When, a few days after Hynde's infamous remarks, ITV's *Loose Women* show had a poll asking whether rape was ever a woman's fault, the very question was denounced as offensive, 'off the scale of acceptability'. Rape Crisis England & Wales tweeted that it was 'not an appropriate opinion poll; legally and morally the answer is a resounding "no"'. The group's national spokesperson, Katie Russell, seemed to believe the media should become a propaganda tool for her own organisation:

> A programme like *Loose Women* could choose to use its
> high profile to raise awareness and understanding of rape,
> its impacts and prevalence, and to support and encourage
> survivors to seek services like those Rape Crisis offers;
> instead, they've reinforced myths and stereotypes with
> this ill-considered, insensitive and insulting poll.[45]

Inevitably, ITV backed off and accepted that 'the wording of the online poll was misjudged and we apologise for any offence caused'. Only a year earlier, TV presenter and national treasure Judy Finnigan was forced to apologise when she talked about convicted rapist Ched Evans and said the rape was 'not violent': 'I apologise unreservedly for any offence that I may have caused as a result of the wording I used.'[46]

Rape is just one of a number of topics now considered taboo. There is an increasing range of issues that are given special protection from scrutiny, where

---

45 'ITV apologises over *Loose Women* rape poll', BBC News, 2 September 2015

46 For a fuller account of the silencing effect of 'rape culture discourse', see the important book by Luke Gittos, *Why Rape Culture is a Dangerous Myth: From Steubenville to Ched Evans* (Exeter: Imprint Academic, 2015)

any deviance from the 'right answer' is denounced as offensive and where those who don't parrot the line are smeared. But every time we accept that certain subjects are taboo or every time someone is made to recant, the rest of us know we are being told to be careful about what we say, and who we offend.

It's not what you said

One famous case shows that the witch-hunters can pillory people wilfully, even for what they did not say. In June 2015, 72-year-old biochemist professor Sir Tim Hunt was forced to resign from an unpaid honorary position at UCL and from a senior position at the Royal Society. A winner of the Nobel Prize in Physiology or Medicine suffered humiliation and disgrace and was turned overnight into a pariah, traduced as a misogynist, because he committed an offence crime. A few short remarks he made one lunchtime in South Korea were interpreted by a small minority of journalists present, led by City University journalism lecturer Connie St Louis, as so sexist that they would hold back a whole generation of young women from becoming scientists. Professor Hunt's infamous 'trouble with girls' speech, in which he talked of the three things that happen when girls are in the lab – 'You fall in love with them, they fall in love with you, and when you criticise them, they cry' – hit headlines worldwide when dubbed as dangerous misogyny.

It is now widely understood that Tim Hunt was unfairly demonised, misquoted, and his words taken out of context. Jonathan Foreman writes in his thorough exposition of the affair that Professor Hunt's 'most ardent persecutors have been exposed as liars or blinkered ideologues, abetted by cynical hacks and academic rivals on a quest to bring him down or use him as grist to a political mill'.[47] Professor Dame Athene Donald, Master of Churchill College, Cambridge, one of Britain's most respected female scientists, has denounced the destruction of Hunt's reputation as 'sloppy journalism fuelled by self-righteous fervour'.

---

47 Jonathan Foreman, 'The Timothy Hunt Witch Hunt: A joke told, a reputation destroyed', Commentary, 1 September 2015

As the truth has been revealed, and the nominal case against him debunked as misreporting at best,[48] it has become obvious that Professor Hunt was vilified not only for comments he didn't make but for patriarchal opinions that he didn't hold. Hunt's final remarks were conveniently never mentioned by his accusers, possibly because they make clear his previous comments were light-hearted. He in fact said: 'Now seriously, I'm impressed by the economic development of Korea. And women scientists played, without doubt, an important role in it. Science needs women, and you should do science despite the obstacles and despite monsters like me!' Indeed, Hunt has a track record as a champion of female scientists, and was at the time of the offence helping the European Research Council develop its 'gender-equity plan'. This should have been enough context to avoid the knee-jerk accusation of misogyny.

But context, intention and humour are no longer a valid defence in today's offence wars. If only Tim Hunt

---

48 The truth of what really occurred in Seoul has been revealed by former Conservative MP Louise Mensch's blog, Unfashionista.com, through admirable and painstaking crowdsourcing of facts and evidence

had understood that it doesn't matter whether *you* know what you mean: there are those 'enlightened ones' who know better how to interpret what your words *really* mean. So even when Hunt's critics concede that he may have been joking, they obstinately insist that his words were harmful regardless. Uta Frith, the chair of the Royal Society's Diversity Committee, wrote that 'as the case of Tim Hunt has shown, prejudice is unacceptable even if meant in jest'.[49] MIT's Deborah Blum adamantly demanded that 'this unfortunate incident must not be portrayed as a private story told as a joke'.[50] And, as far as Hunt's opponents are concerned, even if he didn't mean to be sexist, he was still guilty of unconscious bias.

The notion of unconscious bias, regardless of intent, is now promoted by proponents of the newly emerging microaggressions industry, which is eating its way through free speech on campus and beyond.

---

49 Uta Frith, 'Phoenix not dinosaur', In Verba, 29 June 2015

50 Uta Frith, 'Sexist Scientist: I Was Being "Honest"', The Daily Beast, 16 June 2015

The way microaggressions 'theory' goes, if you add up minor or micro instances of even unconscious racist, homophobic, anti-Semitic, classist, ableist, cissexist speech and behaviour, all these innocuous transgressions give you justifiable reason to feel macro-aggrieved. Everyday Feminism's Aliya Khan explains that: 'The hard thing about microaggressions is that, in many cases, they are entrenched in our culture and society. That means they sneak into our minds and out of our mouths without us being completely aware.' This implies, regardless of what we intend, that our unconscious works against us. And as we are all prone to such misspeaking, Khan notes that 'anyone – from your fellow activist to your kind aunt – is capable of engaging in microaggressions'.[51]

If activists and aunts can be microaggressors, then the rest of us are doomed and Tim Hunt didn't stand a chance. In another article addressed to men, 'You Don't Have to Hate Women to Be Sexist: Everyday Ways You

51   Aliya Khan, '6 Ways to Respond to Sexist Microaggressions in Everyday Conversations', Everyday Feminism, 18 January 2015

May Be Sexist Without Knowing It', it becomes clear what we are up against:

> So you're a man and you consider yourself an awesome ally to women. You may even identify as a feminist and actively work to further the movement's goals. That's all great, but it doesn't give you a pass when it comes to sexism – and you may be perpetuating it without even knowing it … Many times, your unconscious thoughts, actions, and words are still sexist because sexism is often caught up in the subtle things you do without even realising you do them.[52]

One clear message from the Tim Hunt affair is that we must all watch what we say in all circumstances because our words can be taken out of context and, if someone decides to be offended, then you can indeed be labelled offensive. This effectively means that we no longer control our own language and are all prey to malign interpretation. This has a chilling effect. Indeed, when discussing the Tim

---

52 Ally Boguhn, 'You Don't Have to Hate Women to Be Sexist: Everyday Ways You May Be Sexist Without Knowing It', Everyday Feminism, 29 December 2014

Hunt issue on the radio as the story broke, I started to say that perhaps his remarks were 'off colour'. I actually backed away from the phrase 'off colour' and mumbled something incomprehensible. I panicked that perhaps the phrase might be breaking some linguistic code. After all, hadn't actor Benedict Cumberbatch recently been hauled over the coals and suffered an online backlash for using the word 'coloured' in a US television interview, even though he was in fact advocating more prominent roles for black actors? So just the word 'colour' made me twitchy. Ridiculous, I know, and yet the sense of constantly checking language, of trying to anticipate how what we say, however innocently, might be 'called out' (often maliciously) and used against us regardless of our intention, is now part of the way we live, effectively tongue-tying us into muted, sanitised, pre-prepared spin. Scarily, this is backed up by hate speech legislation,[53] which says that

---

53 See, for example, Section 18 of the Public Order Act 1986 that criminalises speech likely to stir racial hatred whether or not the speaker intended the speech to be interpreted as such. Further, offences can be 'racially aggravated' on the basis of how a complainant experienced the speech rather than what the speaker intended. http://www.legislation.gov.uk/ukpga/1986/64/section/18

if anybody interprets any word or view as racist then it is, regardless of the intention of the 'offender'. This privileging of subjective interpretation means we are all easy targets for being accused of hate crime.

Once we sideline the context of speech, common-sense communication becomes dangerously prey to madness and even more bans. It helps explain why certain words are deemed dangerous per se. Deborah Blum's interpretation of one word's meaning predisposed her to find offence, noting in relation to Hunt's speech that 'the word "girl" tends to be a signal flare, a red light warning of problems ahead'. This approach to language can lead to ludicrous situations, such as the arrest of Tottenham Hotspur fans for a racially aggravated public order offence because they call *themselves* the 'Yid Army'. Black American comedian Reginald D. Hunter was effectively accused of racism for an ironic use of the word 'nigger' at an after-dinner speech at the Professional Footballers Association (PFA) awards. So we end up with the bizarre spectacle of the white PFA chair apologising for an anti-racist joke, told by a black comedian, to 'everyone who was offended – and everyone who wasn't'.

We can't even discuss such controversies once context is ignored. Once, in debating the controversy around former *Top Gear* presenter Jeremy Clarkson's alleged mumbling of the n-word in a BBC out-take, I simply referred to the nursery rhyme's first sentence, 'Eeny, meeny, miny, moe…' But this was enough for me to be officially castigated while a member of the audience queried my status as a panellist on Radio 4's *Moral Maze*, quoting the then deputy leader of the Labour Party Harriet Harman's threat: 'Anybody who uses the n-word in public or private in whatever context has no place in the British Broadcasting Corporation.' I remembered Clarkson's remark at the time: 'I've always thought I'd be sacked for something I said. Not for something that, actually, I *didn't* say.'

Toxic victimhood

While what we say is subject to prescription, and the interpretation usurped by others, who is given permission to speak is also a key part of the offence industry. Asserting your especially hurt feelings as a victim can usually allow your opinion to go unchallenged. That omnipresent phrase, 'as a female/Muslim/person of colour/trans person, I find that offensive', is all too often used as a way of silencing opponents. Claiming to be a victim gives people perverse authority. Subjective experience becomes key: 'I am a sexual abuse victim. I am allowed to speak on this. You are not because you have never experienced what it is like to be…' Victim status can buy special privileges and gives the green light to brand opposing views or even mild criticism as tantamount to hate speech. So councils, who have become chief cheerleaders for policing subjective complaints, define hate speech as including 'any behaviour, verbal abuse or insults, offensive leaflets, posters, gestures *as perceived by the victim* or any other person as being motivated by hostility, prejudice or hatred' (my emphasis). This effectively incites 'victims' to shout offence and expect a clampdown. Equally chilling, if a victim aggressively accuses you of offence, it is dangerous to argue back, or even to request that they should stop being so hostile, should you be accused of 'tone policing', a new rule that dictates: '[Y]ou can never question the efficacy of anger … when

voiced by a person from a marginalised background.'[54]
No wonder people are queuing up to self-identify into
any number of victim camps: you can get your voice
heard loudly, close down debate and threaten critics.

What also makes victimhood an attractive currency
today is that it can gain sympathy, as though it is itself
an achievement. And playing the victim is no minority sport. Just watch *The X Factor*. Simon Cowell is no
fool, and the stage-managed background stories that
are now as important as singing ability are a persistent
feature of this and all reality TV shows. Everyone who
has bought into the wider victim sensitivity knows that
revealing desperate hardships – overcoming adversity,
a parent's job loss, family deaths, tales of homelessness
and addiction – all gain brownie points for suffering that
can buy you the sympathy vote. This trend inevitably
encourages an unhealthy awareness of one's own vulnerability, which in turn fuels the desire to claim hurt
as a route to special pleading.

---

54 This and a range of speech-policing devices are discussed comprehensively
by Jonathan Chait in 'Not a Very P.C. Thing to Say', *New York Magazine*,
26 January 2015

In the politicised version, oppressed groups, historically denied equal rights, are now cast – and are often casting themselves – as perennial victims. The progressive demands for universal equal treatment, encompassed in past fights against racism and in support of women's liberation and the decriminalisation of homosexuality, have degenerated into this apolitical, victim-privileging form over the past thirty years. This came to pass largely due to the way that political struggles, which formally united people across cultural, gender, ethnic and religious divisions, have transformed into battles over fragmentary cultural recognition that use victimhood as a currency for attention, resources and even power.

This is exemplified in the way multiculturalism has usurped anti-racism.[55] Over recent decades, as state funding became linked to these cultural identities, different groups began to assert their particular identities more fiercely, with ever greater emphasis on their victim status.

---

55 See Kenan Malik's comprehensive writings critiquing multiculturalism on his blog, Pandaemonium

A group of women artists I knew in the '90s told me a story that will be familiar to many. Turned down for funding as an art collective, they successfully reapplied as the South East Asian Women's art collective. In the following funding round, they were advised to reapply as the Muslim Women's art collective (even though most considered themselves as secular). They got the money, but at a price. Many of the non-religious members left the group altogether and those who remained focused their artistic output on the problems of Islamophobia to merit being considered for future funding.

Today, these identity politics trends are so embedded there is little need for the incentive of funding to encourage the pragmatic relabelling of oneself as part of a cultural victim group. There has been an explosion of different groups vying with one another for recognition and demanding respect. Even terms of abuse are competitive. No sooner do we have 'mansplaining' than someone declares the main problem is 'whitesplaining' or 'straightsplaining.' US writer Cathy Young argues this has led to a 'reverse caste system in which a person's status and worth depends entirely on their perceived oppression and disadvantage'. This in turn creates what *The Atlantic*'s Jonathan Rauch calls the 'offendedness sweepstakes'. There are regular feuds over 'intersectionality'[56] and 'hierarchies of oppression', with internecine warfare between 'TERFs' and the 'trans community', between black women and white feminists, middle-class lesbians and working-class men. Professor emeritus at the University of British Columbia Graham Good, author of *Humanism Betrayed: Theory, Ideology, and Culture in the Contemporary University*, talks of 'the New Sectarianism', which claims its aim is equality, yet assumes superiority for victims with the most disadvantage points, hence turning 'checking privilege' into a routine pastime. And all of this tends to centre on whose voice is most authentic. Just *who* has the right to silence *whom*?

But what happens if you do not possess enough evidence of oppression to compete in the unsavoury scramble for virtuous victim status? Well, one solution is to make more

---

56 Ava Vidal, '"Intersectional feminism". What the hell is it? (And why you should care)', *Daily Telegraph*, 15 January 2014

of less – to magnify the trivial into evidence of major suffering. Take, for example, the UK's Everyday Sexism Project, which encourages women to email in 'instances of sexism experienced', making no distinction between the 'serious or minor, outrageously offensive' or just 'so niggling and normalised that you don't even feel able to protest'. If you think this is ludicrous, this itself is seen as proof of a lack of understanding. This is where microaggression theory is so useful – it allows proponents to keenly explain how '*subtle* digs and biases' (my emphasis), including 'something like a man rolling his eyes when a woman speaks'[57] is evidence you're a victim. The everyday normality of such 'suffering' is emphasised. Derald Wing Sue, in his Psychology Today blog, explains that these

> everyday verbal, nonverbal, and environmental slights,
> snubs, or insults, whether intentional or unintentional
> … may on the surface appear quite harmless, trivial, or
> be described as 'small slights', but research indicates they

---

57 'College Campuses Are Full of Subtle Racism and Sexism, Study Says', Huffington Post, 1 December 2015

have a powerful impact upon the psychological well-being of marginalised groups and affect their standard of living by creating inequities in health care, education, and employment.[58]

Those without sufficient victim status often try to compensate by overzealously empathising with victim groups, as though other people's suffering might rub off some credibility. This explains the escalating trend for some especially privileged liberals to be especially offended *on behalf of* victim groups and dress this up as a form of social justice political activism. This is particularly an issue among those traditionally associated with left-wing movements, as Jamie Bartlett, director of the Centre for the Analysis of Social Media at cross-party think tank Demos, explains in his essay on the topic: '[B]ecause progressives are, or should be, in the business of helping marginalised or oppressed groups', there is an assumption of 'superior virtue or presumed authority to

---

58 Derald Wing Sue, 'Microaggressions: More than Just Race', *Psychology Today*, 17 November 2010

those who are victimised, and a reluctance to disagree with anyone who claims to feel like a victim'.[59]

We have seen the disastrous consequences of this over-compensation of late. An unwillingness to criticise migrants has chilled discussion and paralysed intervention in instances such as the orchestrated sexual exploitation of young girls in Rotherham and Oldham. It also seems to have been a factor in the Swedish authorities' cover-up of widespread sexual assaults by immigrant gangs at a Stockholm music festival in 2015. And it leads to increasing self-censorship, too. I write for the *MJ* (*Municipal Journal*) and so can tell you that the apocryphal stories of ban-happy leftie councils, hyper-attuned to appeasing cultural grievance, are not figments of tabloid writers' imaginations. Well-meaning but defensive local authorities regularly bend over backwards to second guess offence on behalf of mythical victims, even when cultural and religious groups themselves have not complained.

This trend took its most grotesque form when six

---

59 Jamie Bartlett, 'The dangerous allure of victim politics', Little Atoms, 21 August 2015

writers withdrew as literary hosts from the PEN American Center's major annual fundraising gala in New York City in May 2015. Keen to be associated with offended victims, these literary figures argued against the decision to give the Freedom of Expression Courage Award to *Charlie Hebdo*. The weasel excuse that Peter Carey, Michael Ondaatje, Francine Prose, Teju Cole, Rachel Kushner and Taiye Selasi gave for their boycott of the star-studded event was that they were offended on behalf of 'France's vulnerable Muslim minority' (as though they were a uniform, homogenous 'community'). Rachel Kushner said she was withdrawing out of discomfort with what she called the magazine's 'cultural intolerance' and promotion of 'a kind of forced secular view'. Teju Cole claimed that the magazine 'has gone specifically for racist and Islamophobic provocations'. Peter Carey talked of 'PEN's seeming blindness to the cultural arrogance of the French nation, which does not recognise its moral obligation to a large and disempowered segment of their population'. This all followed on from some particularly gross criticism of his fellow cartoonists by Garry Trudeau, creator of the *Doonesbury* comic strip, for 'attacking a powerless, disenfranchised minority with crude, vulgar drawings closer to graffiti than cartoons'. *Charlie*, he said 'wandered into the realm of hate speech'. *Charlie Hebdo* staff, it seems, deserved it.

Toxic identity

Once victimhood becomes such a valued social commodity, it leads to a desperate search for it. Writer and historian Ian Buruma, professor of democracy and human rights at Bard College, writing presciently as long ago as 1999, hints that the 'privileged' can be rather envious 'that they too can't be victims of similarly sufficient magnitude'.[60] I have noticed something similar, when often highly advantaged, privately educated students desperately root around history looking for a personal claim to victimhood. There are comfortably off, black and minority ethnic (BME) youths who suddenly emerge demanding reparations for their ancestors' anguish under

---

60 Ian Buruma, 'The Joys and Perils of Victimhood', *New York Review of Books*, 8 April 1999

slavery, to assuage their own pain. I have Irish friends who claim they are still suffering the consequences of Britain's colonial famine and in all seriousness assert that an official apology would help *them* 'bring closure'.

The row over the statue of Cecil Rhodes at Oxford University also seems a useful vehicle to bolster contemporary personal claims of suffering. Nearly 200 especially privileged international students at Oxford University signed a statement saying that being in receipt of the prestigious Rhodes scholarship 'does not buy their silence', adding that Rhodes's legacy of enforced racial segregation in South Africa '*continues* to alienate, silence, exclude and dehumanise in unacceptable ways' (my emphasis). They even claimed that many among them – 'particularly those of colour, or female, or of African descent, from southern Africa or the former colonies' – took a Rhodes grant as a form of reparation, 'knowing that Cecil Rhodes did not intend it for us when he wrote his will'.[61] What rebels!

---

[61] 'Oxford scholars reject hypocrisy claims amid row over Cecil Rhodes statue', *The Guardian*, 13 January 2016

Once it becomes advantageous to find a victim trump card through a link to ancestral slavery, or to claim past racial segregation as indivisible from gaining a scholarship to an elite university, we may be less surprised at the bizarre story of Rachel Dolezal. Here was a woman who built her entire career as an African-American civil rights activist before she was infamously exposed by her parents in 2015 as having been born Caucasian. Since then, outspoken Black Lives Matter leader Shaun King, the scourge of white privilege, has also been disgraced after his own supporters conceded that his birth certificate shows he is himself white, despite passing as a person of colour.

Author Michelle Malkin argues that cashing in on the 'cult of oppression chic' has been institutionalised. She says that 'race-based affirmative action' in American colleges has groomed 'a cadre of professional minority fakers and fraudsters for decades'. She notes that Dolezal, after receiving a full art scholarship based on her portfolio of 'exclusively African-American portraiture' reportedly encountered anti-white bigotry from campus officials, who had assumed she was black when she applied. According to her family, Dolezal began to make her transition to 'identify as black' after she lost a lawsuit against the university in which she described an atmosphere 'permeated with discriminatory intimidation, ridicule and insult' for being white. As Malkin notes wryly, 'If you can't beat 'em, join 'em.'[62]

So, whereas in the past, gaining access to power may have involved ethnic minorities trying to disguise their colour (like Philip Roth's Coleman Silk, protagonist of *The Human Stain*), now it is the disavowal of one's own biological whiteness that is deemed necessary to becoming a powerful leader or to be given legitimacy to speak authentically about oppression. Dolezal's additional exaggerations of being a victim of a litany of unsubstantiated hate crimes just shows the allure of victimhood these days.

There was some confusion about how to treat Rachel Dolezal's claims to be black after her whiteness was revealed. Some anti-racist activists were scathing

---

62 Michelle Malkin, 'How US campus culture gave us Rachel Dolezal', *New York Post*, 19 June 2015

about her 'cultural appropriation' as 'a glaring example of white privilege in action'. But in an era in which self-defining your identity can be a major free-speech issue (as those who refused to accede to Bradley Manning's demand to be called Chelsea Manning know to their cost), who are we to argue against her stance that she 'identifies' as black? Is this any different from the demand for public applause for Caitlyn Jenner – once known as Olympic athlete Bruce Jenner – who now self-defines as a woman?

This confusion came to the fore early in 2015 when the NUS Women's Conference passed a much-discussed motion – presumably targeted at rugby club blokes donning stilettos – encouraging 'unions to ban clubs and societies from holding events which permit or encourage (cisgender) members to use "cross-dressing" as a mode of fancy dress'. Less commented on but more important was a second statement criticising white gay men from appropriating black female culture by emulating the mannerisms and speech patterns of black women. The NUS quoted Sierra Mannie's article in *Time* magazine, 'Dear White Gays: Stop Stealing Black Female

Culture': '[Y]ou are not a black woman, and you do not get to claim either blackness or womanhood. It is not yours. It is not for you.'[63] Writer Richard Seymour worries that these prescriptions are a form of identity absolutism: 'The premise appears to be that there is an authentic identification rooted in a real, collective lived experience which is being purloined inauthentically by groups who, lacking that experience, do not have a legitimate claim to that identity.'[64]

Confused? You may well be. No wonder we are in a muddle about who has sufficient authenticity to speak on what, whose victimhood outranks whose privilege. Once speech is caught up in this mire, we all end up stifled, unable to comment above and beyond our own narrow experiences, and even then these experiences are subject to authenticity checking. As the Chrissie Hynde story illustrates, there are a range of caveats imposed on who exactly can claim to be a legitimate victim. Unless

---

63 Sierra Mannie, 'Dear White Gays: Stop Stealing Black Female Culture', *Time*, 9 July 2014

64 Richard Seymour, 'The deadlock of identity essentialism', Lenin's Tomb, 26 March 2015

you are a rape victim who repeats the orthodox version of events, you don't count. In fact, you become part of the problem, it seems.

Prescriptive hypocrisy is rife. When constitutional historian Professor David Starkey's alleged racist opinions led to him being edited out of Cambridge University's fundraising video, he was denounced by one PhD activist, Lola Olufemi, in *Varsity* as a white man who 'has never had to question his own profound privilege'.[65] Is that the same Starkey who was raised 'in an austere and frugal environment of near poverty', whose parents were often unemployed, whose mother was a cotton weaver and a cleaner? Is this the same Starkey who was born with two club feet, who suffered polio as a child? Those who succeeded in airbrushing him from the PR video also conveniently failed to mention his homosexuality. His critics might retort that his lowly background or sexuality is irrelevant to his views on multiculturalism. Indeed, they are. In which case, denouncing him

---

65 Lola Olufemi, 'The David Starkey problem with our publicity', *Varsity*, 2 November 2015

as privileged because he is a white professor should be irrelevant to how we assess those views too.

Heavyweight champion boxer Tyson Fury was widely denounced for his homophobic and sexist views when nominated for the BBC's Sports Personality of the Year Award in December 2015. A petition on Change. org – that now fashionable silencing device – attempted to remove him from the shortlist. Those queuing up to defend offended victims from Fury's views overlooked his own claim to victimhood as an 'Irish Traveller', a group that in other identity disputes is embraced by liberal victim-huggers as 'a distinct Irish ethnic minority'. Fury himself knows only too well that being a traveller can mean being treated as a second-class citizen. Several years ago, he told *Boxing News*: 'We're nothing in this society ... no better than dirt on people's shoes. We can be shoved around ... We can be abused because we have no rights.'[66] But when he more recently came under attack for his views on women and homosexuality, the boxer refused to play the victim card. Asked

66 Nigel Collins, 'Fury's roots echo familiar story', ESPN, 9 January 2013

what he thought about those who signed the petition, he jeered: '50,000 wankers. That's what I say about them … They can suck my balls.'

I am glad that Hynde, Starkey and Fury refused to play along with the defensive 'my emotional scars are bigger than yours' game of victimhood one-upmanship. But too many do as a way to silence others. This has become a common strategy on social media, where so many free-speech disputes now play out on full volume.

Toxic Twitter

Most of the offence controversies I have described either started on, or at least were hugely amplified by, social media. However, I am wary of indulging in techno-determinism by blaming Twitter for undermining free speech. But I do concede that the prevalence of virtual moral panics and 'twitchmob' rule do have a silencing effect. Many people are scared that their reputations and careers might be at risk if uttering the 'wrong' word or 'wrong' views stir up the wrath of Twittermobs. Jon Ronson's book *So You've Been Publicly Shamed* has received widespread (and well-deserved) plaudits, as it so accurately captures the recognisable viciousness of this climate. American political commentator Rebecca Traister wrote in 2014: 'All over social media, there dwell armies of unpaid but widely read commentators, ready to launch hashtag campaigns and circulate Change.org petitions in response to the slightest of identity-politics missteps.'[67]

But who are the online culprits we should blame for free-speech transgressions, and who are the victims? It is not as simple as sometimes assumed.

Some people uncritically reel off a now well-rehearsed script and claim that women – obviously – are the main victims. So the former shadow Home Secretary Yvette Cooper (a woman who has had some of the most powerful jobs in British politics) is fronting a new campaign called 'Reclaim the Internet' that aims to prevent women from being 'drowned out by vitriol and hate'. The argument goes that trolls are so intimidating that women's

---

67 Rebecca Traister, 'A Woman Should Run for President Against Hillary Clinton. Or Many Women', *New Republic*, 26 June 2014

free speech online is under threat. Cooper declares: 'Unless misogyny on the internet is challenged, more women's voices will be silenced, and more women will be oppressed or feel prevented from speaking out just as if we'd gone back to the Victorian age.' But when she patronisingly casts women as particularly unable to withstand nasty tweets, however aggressive, she ends up repeating the sexist Victorian trope about women being the feeble fairer sex.

Of course, some abuse on Twitter is unbelievably vile and relentless and the caricatured trolls can be obnoxious and foul-mouthed. But it is ultimately just words uttered by a bunch of pathetic saddos. Even Cooper admits that being trolled is not quite as traumatic as often described: 'In the end this isn't about experienced politicians like me, Liz [Kendall], Stella [Creasy], Angela [Eagle], Caroline [Flint] or Harriet [Harman]. We're never going to be silenced by the high-tech equivalent of angry letters written in green ink that politicians have received for centuries.' Instead, she patronisingly assumes that mere mortal girls might be put off: 'The real concern is if young women in particular end up feeling like that they have to censor themselves on social media because of the abuse that they might get.'[68]

If we dig a bit deeper, we discover it is rather more complicated. As Jamie Bartlett explains in his book *The Dark Net*, complaining about trolls is increasingly deployed as a weapon in gaining further sympathy as a Victim with a capital 'V': 'Being trolled by strangers on the net gives you the chance to show how hard things are for you, how right you were, and how noble and magnanimous you are in sharing your suffering with the world.' How has Connie St Louis responded to criticism of her shoddy and irresponsible behaviour in launching an international Twitter witch-hunt against Professor Tim Hunt? With zero self-awareness she incessantly whinges about an online witch-hunt against *her*: 'Women are vulnerable to vicious trolling on Twitter … and black women doubly so.'

Those who grumble that women are being driven away from social media often seem to be demanding special

---

68 'Sexist online trolls are putting women off joining Labour, warns failed leadership candidate Yvette Cooper', *Daily Mail*, 26 September 2015

gender immunity from criticism, branding those who won't oblige as 'trolls' and those who persistently argue back as harassers. One recent spat illustrates the murky mess. In January 2016, Twitter plc put Milo Yiannopoulos, tech editor at Breitbart.com, on the naughty step by removing his 'blue tick' verification. Yiannopoulos, known internationally as @Nero, isn't to everyone's taste; certainly Jessie Thompson, editorial assistant at HuffPost UK Blogs, is no fan: 'He's kind of like Katie Hopkins except he's never come second on *Celebrity Big Brother* … he thinks feminists are "bullies", and was an advocate for GamerGate … He's basically a professional troll.'[69] But being a GamerGate supporter or being infamous for scathing, sharp-tongued and unapologetic attacks on PC feminists, even calling them bullies, are perfectly legitimate political opinions. Labelling such disagreements as trolling has serious consequences for free speech.

Indeed, complaints about being a 'troll victim' are invariably accompanied by demands for more censorship.

---

69 Jessie Thompson, 'Thank You Twitter – By Unverifying Milo Yiannopoulos, You Are Standing Up for Women Online', Huffington Post, 9 January 2016

When comedian Kate Smurthwaite appeared on the *Today* programme to back up Yvette Cooper's campaign, she urged that the police set up a special squad to monitor Twitter and punish sexist trolls accordingly. But when feminists demand that the police arrest and even imprison trolls to create an online safe space for women, it is they who become the authoritarian silencers of others. They are legitimising, in effect, 'thought-crime'.

We should at least acknowledge that it is not easy to see who the victims and the bullies are on Twitter. Perversely, social media is where the most vicious and unrelenting civil war between (rather than against) feminists, is taking place, as the new women's movement(s) splinter into ever pettier, narrow identity grouplets. In her fascinating, if depressing, article 'Feminism's Toxic Twitter Wars', Michelle Goldberg gives a litany of gruesome examples: '[M]any of the most avid digital feminists will tell you that [Twitter has] become toxic. Indeed, there's a nascent genre of essays by people who feel emotionally savaged by their involvement in it – not because of sexist trolls, but because of the slashing righteousness of other feminists.' Goldberg quotes

Courtney Martin, who, when she organised a conference to leverage support for online feminism, received such vitriolic reactions from other feminists 'it felt like some sort of Maoist hazing'. Former Feministing.com editor Samhita Mukhopadhyay told Goldberg: 'Everyone is so scared to speak right now.'[70]

Toxic campus

When feminists start declaring they are too scared to speak because of other feminists, we can really begin to see how toxic today's identity-driven, 'I find that offensive' disputes have become. And there is nowhere more potently symbolic of this toxicity than on campus, which has become the key arena for fostering the most pernicious weapons against free speech and the place where today's trends towards being easily offended are most visible and most grotesquely played out.

Things are becoming serious. When University

---

70 Michelle Goldberg, 'Feminism's Toxic Twitter Wars', *The Nation*, 29 January 2014

College London's Students' Union banned the Nietzsche Society because it threatened 'the safety of the UCL student body', we might wonder what other philosophers are for the chop and whether the pursuit of knowledge itself can survive the onslaught. One key culprit to blame for the new phenomenon of philistine censorship is trigger warnings, those red flags that tell students that course content might trigger 'a traumatic effect in response to their own personal experiences if texts contain scenes of domestic violence, sexism, racism...' This means students can choose not to be taught huge chunks of necessary academic material if they anticipate the content might trigger them, making them feel uncomfortable or distressed by triggering memories of a traumatic event. Literature is inevitably in the firing line (all that yukky human condition stuff like sex, death, depravity and emotional intensity). Over the past couple of years, students have called for trigger warnings on classic texts as varied as Virginia Woolf's *Mrs Dalloway*, for its 'suicidal inclinations', to Ovid's *Metamorphoses*, for its 'sexual assaults'.

Merely carrying out the traditional academic work of

intellectual exploration can mean facing accusations of triggering trauma. In a *New Yorker* essay, Harvard Law School professor Jeannie Suk writes about how hard it is to teach rape law in an era of trigger warnings. She explains how women's organisations now 'routinely advise students that they should not feel pressured to attend or participate in class sessions that focus on the law of sexual violence, and which might therefore be traumatic' as they might '"trigger" traumatic memories'. She describes the way many students appear to equate 'the risk ... of a traumatic injury' incurred while discussing sexual misconduct as 'analogous to sexual assault itself'. As a consequence, more and more teachers of criminal law are not including rape law in their courses: 'it's not worth the risk of complaints of discomfort by students' and they fear being accused of inflicting 'emotional injuries' in classroom conversation.[71] Meanwhile, terrifyingly, South African students at the University of Cape Town (the inspiration for

---

71 Jeannie Suk, 'The Trouble with Teaching Rape Law', *New Yorker*, 15 December 2014

Oxford University's #RhodesMustFall campaign) seem to have embraced a racialised agenda, happily burning paintings of white alumni and former academic luminaries in February 2016.[72]

In such an atmosphere, it is no wonder that one American professor, using the pseudonym Edward Schlosser, wrote an essay titled, 'I'm a Liberal Professor, and My Liberal Students Terrify Me'. 'Schlosser' explained that the 'student–teacher dynamic has been reenvisioned' simultaneously along 'consumerist and hyper-protective' lines, giving 'every student the ability to claim Grievous Harm in nearly any circumstance, after any affront, and a teacher's formal ability to respond to these claims is limited at best'.[73] I hear similar complaints from many academics in UK universities, who see their own students as the aggressive perpetrators of offence disputes. They moan that they have to negotiate nervously around too many topics to

---

72 'UCT and #RhodesMustFall: A burning issue', Daily News, 19 February 2016

73 Edward Schlosser, 'I'm a Liberal Professor, and My Liberal Students Terrify Me', Vox, 3 June 2015

avoid offending a generational cohort who hurl around accusations such as whorephobic, transphobic, biphobic and Islamophobic with (gay) abandon. One older academic (by which I mean in his forties) confessed that he felt he needed an offence dictionary even to negotiate the new language etiquette: 'What the hell do "cissexism", "Mx" [and] "non-binary" mean?' There is pressure on staff to conform to student-centred speech codes, anti-harassment policies and safe-space initiatives. How to teach ideas, let alone challenge ideas, in such an atmosphere?

And yet, blaming today's 'cotton-wool kids' can be misplaced. This can mean culpability is aimed at the wrong targets. After all, the notion that words hurt has been the bedrock of radical politics for many years. It is members of my generation of equality activists who campaigned for hate speech legislation, and made 'no platform' censorship a respectable left-wing position, long before today's fragile students were born. Those no-platform-championing radicals I argued against at university in the '80s may have focused on silencing far-right groups such as the National Front, whose 'rhetoric of violence' was said to 'inspire leagues of smash-happy skinheads'[74] rather than today's student unions that promiscuously ban feminists or anyone who dares offend. However, the intellectual origins of blurring the distinction between violent words and actual violence, and censoring ideas for being dangerous, are clear.

But, even knowing this, we still need to more fully understand why today's young seem so particularly likely to be caused distress by being offended, why they lack the resilience to be able to brush off insults or innocuous microaggressions or bounce back from criticism. Why are they so susceptible to being sucked into an ever-spiralling 'vortex of grievance'[75] and sense that words are threatening? It is not as though today's young have been born with an especially weak constitution and a propensity to be offended. In truth, they are *our* creation and learnt the lessons of trigger-happy

---

74 'Nick Lowles, Why "No Platform" means something different today', HOPE not hate, 6 January 2013

75 Steve Stewart-Williams, 'Microaggressions and the New Culture of Victimhood', *Psychology Today*, 8 September 2015

censorship from their elders. So who are the real culprits responsible for Generation Snowflake's fragility?
Let's find out.

Part II

Creating the Snowflake Generation

Socialised into safe spaces

IN NOVEMBER 2015, a short video went viral that showed a confrontation between a Yale faculty head, Nicholas Christakis, and a screaming, almost hysterical mob of students. The video generated such a backlash towards the students' behaviour that they were soon labelled with the disparaging moniker 'Generation Snowflake'. The furore began with a request by the university's Intercultural Affairs Council that Yale students avoid wearing Halloween costumes that could offend minority students, specifically advising people to steer clear of feathered headdresses, turbans or blackface. Christakis's wife, Erika, a lecturer in early childhood education, responded in an email suggesting that everyone should relax a bit rather than labelling fancy dress costumes as 'culturally insensitive'. Rather than heeding these sensible words, however, the students reacted with fury.

Erika Christakis's email is worth reading in full.[76] It is brimming with erudite reflections based on her scholarship as an 'educator concerned with the developmental stages of childhood and young adulthood'. For example, she pointed out that Halloween is 'traditionally a day of subversion for children and young people' and asked if there was room anymore for a young person 'to be a little bit obnoxious … a little bit inappropriate or provocative or, yes, offensive?' (As events turned out, the answer seems to be a resounding 'no' on that front.) She sensibly advised, 'If you don't like a costume someone is wearing, look away, or tell them you are offended. Talk to each other. Free

---

76 'Email from Erika Christakis: "Dressing Yourselves" email to Silliman College (Yale) Students on Halloween Costumes', FIRE, 30 October 2015

speech and the ability to tolerate offence are the hall-marks of a free and open society.'

Yet, the words in this entirely reasonable email made the students feel 'unsafe' and led to the vicious attack levelled at her husband. As detailed in the excellent commentary on the filmed exchange by *The Atlantic*'s Conor Friedersdorf, one student screams: 'In your position as master, it is your job to create a place of comfort and home for the students ... You have not done that. By sending out that email, that goes against your position as master. Do you understand that?!' When he replies, 'No, I don't agree with that', the student explodes:

> Then why the fuck did you accept the position?! Who the fuck hired you?! ... If that is what you think about being a master you should step down! It is not about creating an intellectual space! It is not! Do you understand that? It's about creating a home here. You are not doing that![77]

---

77 Conor Friedersdorf, 'The New Intolerance of Student Activism', *The Atlantic*, 9 November 2015

Here we see that Generation Snowflake students view universities less as the home of knowledge or rational discourse, but just home as in homely. And this is a transatlantic trend. A similar argument was also a justification for the banning of a debate on abortion at Christ Church College, Oxford at the end of 2014. The president of the Cambridge Union, Tim Squirrell, defended the ban: 'Universities are also our homes … it is not only [students'] right to feel safe in a space that they call their home, but it is the obligation of the college to *make* it safe.' Squirrell went on to explain, in a blogpost 'challenging the idea that all weakness is bad', that 'we, as students, are beginning to realise that there is more to life than just discussion … that we don't need to be ashamed of our weaknesses and vulnerabilities … that sometimes we have to prioritise the emotional, mental and physical well-being of our friends and colleagues over the ability of privileged people to come into our homes and say whatever they like'.[78]

This is a remarkable reconceptualisation of what

---

78 Tim Squirrell, 'Why Free Speech isn't absolute and it's okay to be vulnerable', 23 November 2014

it means to be a student, embracing a model of weak, vulnerable home-birds. It was not that long ago that I could guarantee a laugh from student audiences when I described a higher education access initiative called 'Feel at home days', a pathetic scheme to encourage pupils from non-traditional backgrounds to attend universities. Advocates of this type of approach suggested that aspects of university life – such as gowns and ritual, lectures and tutorials – might be alienating. The conclusion was that higher education institutions should adapt and reassure would-be recruits that university was just an extension of school and home. When I talked about this a few years ago, students would share the joke about such a ludicrous and patronising notion. They recognised that the very point of going to university was to escape home, to get away from small-town preoccupations, the limits of spoon-fed lessons, *in loco parentis* teachers and being looked after. The very excitement of undergraduate life was that it represented a completely different experience from school, precisely a break from home comforts. A rite of passage, undergraduate life could be a period of relatively grown-up freedom and independence; it was about standing on your own two feet, a time full of alien but exciting social and intellectual adventures.

How things have changed. It is now students who demand that campus feels like home. In *The Spectator*, the editor of spiked, Brendan O'Neill (one of the banned debaters from Oxford), wrote:

> If your go-to image of a student is someone who's free-spirited and open-minded, who loves having a pop at orthodoxies, then you urgently need to update your mind's picture bank. Students are now pretty much the opposite of that. It's hard to think of any other section of society that has undergone as epic a transformation as students have. From free-wheelin' to ban-happy, from askers of awkward questions to suppressors of offensive speech, in the space of a generation.[79]

Of course, when students demand to be made to feel comfortable and safe on campus, this is not a physical

---

79 Brendan O'Neill, 'Free speech is so last century. Today's students want the "right to be comfortable"', *The Spectator*, 22 November 2014

matter. Following Erika Christakis's Halloween email furore, several students complained that they felt so unsafe they wanted to move away from living at Silliman College as they were 'losing sleep … skipping meals … having breakdowns'. Yet, as Friedersdorf points out, this was despite enjoying very real material comforts:

> These are young people who live in safe, heated buildings with two Steinway grand pianos, an indoor basketball court, a courtyard with hammocks and picnic tables, a computer lab, a dance studio, a gym, a movie theater, a film-editing lab, billiard tables, an art gallery and four music practice rooms. But they can't bear this setting that millions of people would risk their lives to inhabit because one woman wrote an email that hurt their feelings?

Safety is now redefined in more existential terms, as being protected from offence or upsetting ideas. Formal safe-space policies often promise a judgement-free environment, guaranteed by excluding views that challenge a pre-given consensus. When the Christ Church Junior Common Room lobbied the college to reconsider holding the debate on abortion, it was on the basis of the damage it could do to the 'emotional and mental well-being' of the college students. Niamh McIntyre, one of the organisers against the debate, explained: 'As a student, I asserted that it would make me feel threatened in my own university.' What sort of threat? That 'words and views might hurt women'.[80]

As such, safe spaces have become an incontrovertible threat to free speech. So much so that the University of Manchester Students' Union stopped its Free Speech and Secularist Society from handing out copies of a specially produced memorial edition of *Charlie Hebdo* at the university's Refreshers' Fair because 'the welcoming event was to be a comfortable and inclusive environment where people should not feel ridiculed'.[81] Meanwhile, the University of Bristol's student union officer Alex Bradbrook said selling the issue 'wouldn't pass our

---

80 Niamh McIntyre, 'I helped shut down an abortion debate between two men because my uterus isn't up for their discussion', *The Independent*, 18 November 2014

81 'Students' Union censors *Charlie Hebdo*', University of Manchester Free Speech and Secular Society blog, 27 January 2015

safe-space policy'. When Kate Smurthwaite clashed with Goldsmiths University Students' Union about the content of her comedy gig, an organiser explained, 'I have to send you a passage about our "safe space" policy outlining kinda what you can or can't say.'[82]

In 2014, Toni Pearce, then president of the National Union of Students, declared: 'I'm really proud that our movement takes safe spaces seriously.' Amusingly, this can get students' unions into their own PC muddle. When ex-Muslim Iranian human-rights campaigner Maryam Namazie gave a talk to Goldsmiths' Atheist, Secularist and Humanist Society, the university's Islamic Society disrupted the event by shouting 'Safe space!' Some thought it bizarre that Goldsmiths Feminist Society issued a statement standing 'in solidarity' with the Islamic Society.[83] Here, hardline feminists sided with hardline Muslims because, they said: 'Safety is our first priority', and agreed with the Islamic brothers' own statement that

---

82 Quoted by Ian Dunt in 'Safe space or free speech? The crisis around debate at UK universities', *The Guardian*, 6 February 2015

83 Goldsmiths Students' Union Feminist Society statement, 2 December 2015

claimed Namazie's talk would 'be a violation to our safe space, a policy which Goldsmiths SU adheres to strictly'.

A feminist organisation allying itself with a group of men who shout down a woman discussing her ideas might suggest there's nothing 'safe' about these spaces anymore. But it also raises another important question: why do the young – historically associated with risk-taking, experimentation, rule-breaking and pushing boundaries – now see safety as a trump-all virtue, so much so that concerns about safety are regularly deployed to censor, ban and retreat from argument? We may be cynical about the authenticity of the Goldsmiths Islamists' desire for safety, but why do so many teenagers and young adults, who as a generation have always been those who aspired to freedom from adult supervision and who regularly rebelled against authority diktat, now demand to live in a hermetically sealed, risk-free cocoon, protected from harm by authority figures who they complain do not police their 'homes' stringently enough?

The short answer is: we socialised them that way. They have been reared on stories about how vulnerable and in need of protection they are. Adult society has fed them a diet of anxieties and provided the language of safety and risk aversion that now threatens liberal values of tolerance and resilience. We are reaping what we have sown – and the young Snowflake Generation, so quick to shout offence, are merely ventriloquising our own fears imposed on them as children.

Health and safety madness

In an excellent essay on the topic, 'The Coddling of the American Mind', Greg Lukianoff, president and CEO of the Foundation for Individual Rights in Education (FIRE) and social psychologist professor Jonathan Haidt discuss some important generational shifts, explaining that 'children born after 1980 – the Millennials – got a consistent message from adults: life is dangerous, but adults will do everything in their power to protect you from harm, not just from strangers'. They describe how childhood itself has changed greatly during the past generation: 'Many Baby Boomers and Gen Xers can remember riding their bicycles around their home-towns, unchaperoned by adults, by the time they were eight or nine years old. In the hours after school, kids were expected to occupy themselves, getting into minor scrapes and learning from their experiences.' But with 'free range' childhood now demonised, many parents have 'pulled in the reins', while '[t]he flight to safety also happened at school. Dangerous play structures were removed from playgrounds; peanut butter was banned from student lunches.'[84]

Lukianoff and Haidt identify something important here. A key to the phenomenon of our thin-skinned society is to understand how a safety-first agenda has been driven by transferring adults' fearful obsessions onto children's lived experience. And, undoubtedly, today's health and safety mania has helped create a new type of young person: kids denied many of the freedoms and escapades, such as playing outdoors, climbing trees and so on, may well be inculcated with a greater sense of timidity, having been warned that the world outside the home is a scary place. So much so that there has recently been something

---

84 Greg Lukianoff and Jonathan Haidt, 'The Coddling of the American Mind', *The Atlantic*, September 2015

of an official backlash against mollycoddling and an awareness that restricting the life experiences of children has created 'cotton-wool kids'. In an article bluntly titled 'A Nation of Wimps', Hara Estroff Marano, editor-at-large of *Psychology Today*, describes a typically American scene:

> Maybe it's the cyclist in the park, trim under his sleek metallic blue helmet, cruising along the dirt path ... at three miles an hour. On his tricycle.
>
> Or perhaps it's today's playground, [the] all-rubber-cushioned surface where kids used to skin their knees. And... wait a minute... those aren't little kids playing. Their mommies – and especially their daddies – are in there with them, coplaying or play-by-play coaching. Few take it half-easy on the perimeter benches, as parents used to do, letting the kids figure things out for themselves.[85]

Marano argues that because parents are going to such ludicrous lengths to take the bumps out of life for their

---

85 Hara Estroff Marano, 'A Nation of Wimps', *Psychology Today*, 1 November 2004; updated 20 November 2015

children, this hyper-concern is having 'the net effect of making kids more fragile'.

These are some of the concerns raised in the 2015 report, *Play*, published by the UK's All-Party Parliamentary Group on a Fit and Healthy Childhood. It calls for some radical changes in our approach to children's play to counter the effects of over-cosseting. Things have gone so far that even politicians, usually so cautious, advocate that adults allow children to go out 'exploring alone with the possibility of getting lost', and to let them play 'near potentially dangerous elements such as water and cliffs'. Hurrah to that. What is more, the report writers identify adult fears as 'the mainspring of the change' in attitudes to play, recognising that a safety-driven approach 'is unlikely to have been instigated by children, who have an inborn urge to push the boundaries and take up challenges'.

Catastrophising life's challenges

Lukianoff and Haidt argue, rightly, that Generation Snowflake engage in 'catastrophising', always anticipating the worst possible outcomes to any number of situations. But they do so by regurgitating the sort of hyped-up scare stories they have learnt growing up. One of the characteristic features of modern society is the normalisation of the hyperbole of catastrophe, with attendant doom-mongering about everything from climate change to the 'ageing timebomb'. All too many of society's present and future challenges are discussed using Hollywood-style, disaster-movie rhetoric. We cower in fear at the 'what ifs' presented by unknown unknowns.

Is it any wonder, then, that kids grow up scared of their own shadow when society is so jumpy? What is more, we project these fears onto children, especially via schools, which are charged with the fool's errand of warning children about the perils of every social problem imaginable, from drugs, obesity and alcohol to political apathy and global warming. Scare stories are also used routinely by NGOs and charities, who insist on always seeing the worst side of every story and then claiming children need even greater protection.

The key point is that this wider mood of risk aversion is far more of a problem than just parents not letting their kids out to ride their bikes. Yet there is much less kick-back about this phenomenon, one in which adult society socialises the young by warning them that *everything* is a risk.

Also, adult society is officially more anxious. According to journalist Sharon Begley, there has been 'an increase in the prevalence of reported anxiety disorders of more than 1,200 per cent since 1980'. She asks: 'In the Age of Anxiety, are we all mentally ill?'[86] This seems to be skewing how adults interpret the quite normal ups and downs of childhood; we seem intent on transposing our own anxieties onto how we view young people's lives and then swamping younger generations with endless threats to their well-being.

Over recent years, a plethora of reports and surveys clamber to tell us that 21st-century children are miserable and facing unprecedented ills and problems. For example, at the start of 2012, newspaper headlines proclaimed 'Unhappy childhoods afflict one in

---

86 Sharon Begley, 'In the Age of Anxiety, are we all mentally ill?', Reuters, 13 July 2012

ten youngsters'. This followed the publication of a 'landmark survey' by the Children's Society of 30,000 eight- to sixteen-year-olds. Elaine Hindal, director of the Society's 'Campaign for Childhood' declared, 'We know that, right now, half a million children are unhappy', and 'unless we act now' we risk creating 'a lost future generation'. Meanwhile, in February 2016, the International Survey of Children's Well-Being (ISCWeB) was trumpeted as proving that eight-year-olds in England are a miserable bunch, less happy than those from Romania or Turkey, leading to a plethora of angsty media features and official soul-searching about why England ranked thirteenth out of sixteen countries.

Such headline-grabbing stats have led to primary school teachers deploying a range of new-age, anxiety-reducing techniques such as aromatherapy, yoga and 'chill out' music into classrooms. Anthony Seldon, when headteacher of Wellington College, became the first in the country to timetable happiness lessons, to counter the gloom (now supplemented by even wackier mindfulness classes). Positive psychology has become all the rage: its guru, US psychologist Professor Martin

Seligman, has been brought over to train British teachers in the art of making our miserable children happier.

But these assertions about miserable children contrast with the objective truth: the great majority of children born into today's developed societies enjoy unprecedented levels of health and safety. Professor David Buckingham, himself the author of a report in 2009 entitled *The Impact of the Commercial World on Children's Wellbeing*, conceded that the fashionable idea of 'toxic childhoods' 'provides an extremely negative representation of contemporary childhood' in which 'children are portrayed as vulnerable and helpless victims, rather than in any way resilient or competent – or indeed happy'. Helpfully, Buckingham noted that we were in danger of neglecting 'the more positive aspects of modern childhood ... The possibility that most children (and their parents) are reasonably well-adjusted and doing fairly well is rarely entertained.' But in the nine years since his report, Buckingham's warnings have largely been drowned out by ever more panics about new problems, such as the sexualisation of childhood, online grooming by jihadists and an intensified exams treadmill, all of which we are told may affect the mental health of the young.

We seem determined to see the glass as half-empty. Even news that the young are more careful, perhaps even overly cautious, when it comes to drinking, drug-taking and promiscuity, is no consolation. Fiona Brooks, head of adolescent and child health at the University of Hertfordshire, says that 'although there has been a decline in traditional risk behaviours like smoking and drug and alcohol abuse, there hasn't been a transition to more positive health behaviours'.[87] Brooks warns instead of a 'ticking timebomb' due to 'the rise in poor mental health among young people' suggesting causes such as 'parents … busy and stressed, and children's lives … becoming more pressurised'.

Similarly, journalist Sam Leith, in an article titled *'Que Sera, Sera?* An Unhappy Life For Our Children', adds to the despair. He also notes that 'the kids aren't drinking, drugging and fornicating as much as we did',

---

87 Quoted in 'Self-harm rate triples among teenagers in England', BBC *Newsbeat*, 21 May 2014

but still goes on to list a frightening series of new woes: 'Instead, they are self-harming, succumbing to depression, developing eating disorders and persecuting each other online.' Leith's critique of grade inflation is that it has increased anxieties 'for children of any ambition' for whom not getting an A* 'is unthinkable, terrifying, life-ending'.[88] I am as worried about 'grade inflation' as anyone, but using language like 'terrifying' and 'life-ending' to talk about kids' exam worries seems likely to reinforce their anxieties rather than teaching them how to cope with exam nerves, even failure and so on. When adults themselves catastrophise about young people's lives in such a way, is it any wonder they grow up believing that every challenge is insurmountable?

The way adults discuss their concerns rubs off onto children, and can affect how they respond to any difficulties they face. Many of the official statistics on children's unhappiness are based on surveys of young people's attitudes. When children as young as five report

---

88 'Que Sera, Sera? An Unhappy Life For Our Children', *Evening Standard*, 5 October 2015

that they are 'stressed' or suffering 'anxiety', or talk of their own 'well-being', did they learn this vocabulary in the playground? Hardly. It suggests they have been trained in, or have at least imbibed, adults' counselling jargon, encouraged from a very young age, by a glut of professionals, to see themselves as emotionally fragile. A constant stream of initiatives that purport to help children deal with 'stress' can too easily become self-perpetuating. So, when the 'Preventing Anxiety in Children through Education in Schools' programme holds lessons in cognitive behavioural therapy (CBT) for children in primary schools, I fear this will encourage children to be self-obsessive about their own interior emotional life, which they will inevitably verbalise as soon as one of the army of opinion poll surveyors asks them 'How do you feel?'

So, children's lives over recent years comprise: being over-protected by a risk-averse, health and safety culture, and being reared in a climate that routinely catastrophises and pathologises both social challenges and young people's state of mind. We might pause here to recognise features of offence disputes later on. It starts to become clear that the origins of today's young adults' belief that they have a right to be protected and need to be kept safe lie in the unintended consequences of specific child protection concerns that now dominate the public imagination.

However, this general, looser atmosphere of fear becomes properly embedded once it takes on the systematic shape of official interventions into young people's lives. And there are several specific policies that fall under the heading of child protection and safeguarding, that seem particularly influential in scaring the young, and are major culprits in shaping Generation Snowflake.

Culprits: public health scares

Invoking children's safety has become a go-to tactic for any organisation lobbying for urgent 'something-must-be-done' interventions. It has become such a cliché that one suspects that every organisation has a pre-prepared 'think of the children' press release on hand for all occasions, nowhere more so than in the arena of health protection. No public health panic, from 'binge drinking' to 'unfit couch potatoes', is complete without emphasising the dangers to young people.

If obsessively worrying about our health has become so pervasive for adults that GPs complain about surgeries clogged up with the 'worried well', focusing on children has inevitably also been anxiety-inducing. They too have become over-preoccupied with threats to their physical well-being.

One particularly pernicious example of how this has happened is the increasing hysteria about an obesity 'epidemic'. There is so little restraint on fearmongering on this issue that the Chief Medical Officer for England Professor Dame Sally Davies used her annual report in December 2015 to call on the government to treat obesity as a 'national threat' on a par with terrorism. Of course, we should expect medical experts to care about children's health. However, we should be wary of frightening the young when we bluntly declare that this generation of children may not live as long as their parents because of an 'obesity timebomb'. With a bit of perspective, we might remember that today's young have unprecedented chances of living long, healthy lives, with one third of babies born in 2013 expected to live to be 100 according to the UK Office for National Statistics. Indeed, we seem to have two apparently contradictory timebombs facing us: one where millions die sooner because of obesity alongside one where people live much longer due to improving healthcare, leading to fears that the cost of pensions and social care will bankrupt the state.

This is not to say there is no problem when it comes to children's weight, diet or fitness. But simplistic moralising to children and their parents about food underestimates the complexities of the issue on which even the experts disagree. Various authors have recently done a real service in unpicking obesity myths and should give us ample evidence for scepticism (for example, see Rob Lyons's book *Panic on a Plate* and Christopher Snowdon's *The Fat Lie*). But, whether urban myth or fact, the metaphorical epidemic of obesity has made young people into objects of professional condescension and established fear as a factor of their everyday eating habits.

Generation Snowflake were those children first

subjected to the government's controversial 'fat charts', involving the mass weighing and measuring of school pupils from the age of four. A whole swathe of anti-obesity initiatives in turn tell the young to become preoccupied with their body shape and food intake. It hardly helps when Labour MP Keith Vaz hysterically declares a 'war on sugar' in Parliament, or the lobby group Action on Sugar proclaims sugar is 'the new tobacco' and 'the alcohol of childhood'. Children are taught they are continually at risk from fizzy drinks, fatty chips and chocolate. On the back of such doomsday scenarios, Generation Snowflake has heard celebrity TV chef Jamie Oliver call their parents 'fucking tossers' for allegedly stuffing their packed lunches with junk food. Their teachers, bolstered by Oliver's sanctimonious insults, preposterously send home notes in lunch boxes to reprimand 'naughty' parents for serving inappropriate snacks to their own children. One school hit the headlines for expelling a six-year-old for bringing Mini Cheddars to school. The key message to the young: be very, very scared of even the food you eat.

And such health zealotry might also give us a clue

about how easily offended young people learn that words and images are so dangerous that they should be banned. Today's public health fearmongering is integrally linked with censorship. In January 2008, Ofcom banned adverts for foods high in fat, salt and sugar in programmes aimed at children under sixteen. Public Health England's report for the House of Commons Health Select Committee, released in October 2015, called for extending that ban to *all* programmes shown before 9 p.m. (an idea backed by the committee's report in November) and regulation of the use of cartoon characters in marketing. There are even calls to ban the Coco Pops monkeys because they dangerously 'engage children and affect food preference and choice'. Meanwhile, Dr Hilary Cass, in her role as president of the Royal College of Paediatrics and Child Health, declared: 'People will argue about the merits or otherwise of giving schools freedom over the curriculum and how children are taught, but when it comes to school food, there can be *no debate* (my emphasis).' No debate, banning adverts, regulating dangerous images – all to protect the young. No wonder children reared on such a censorious diet grow up to repeat these arguments when faced with damaging ideas and publications.

Culprits: child protection

If public health scares encourage children to worry, it is the child protection industry that tips them over into paranoia. It has actively encouraged children to see potential abuse everywhere. One key policy, Every Child Matters, unhelpfully shifted the balance of child protection from a targeted service aimed at protecting the minority to making *all* services relating to *all* children adopt child safety as a central concern.

This has spiralled into an outright moral panic, where society sees sexual abuse and stranger danger everywhere. There is ever more suspicion about innocent behaviour, from the ban on parents taking photos of children at swimming galas to the emergence of child-only parks that allow adults to enter 'only if accompanied by a child'. Criminal records vetting of any adult – as employee or volunteer – regularly coming into contact with children has had an insidious effect on intergenerational trust. What lessons do children learn when no adult dare hug or comfort a crying toddler for fear of that dreaded accusation of 'inappropriate behaviour'?

Fear has been ratcheted up even further after the exposure of the vile crimes perpetrated by TV and radio personality Jimmy Savile, and the escalating number of historic sexual abuse investigations (such as Operation Yewtree) being conducted by multiple police forces throughout the UK. From a rare example of a vicious pervert, we now find that all children's homes, kids' entertainers, music tutors and hospital volunteers are presented as a potential threat to the young. The consequences are intensely paranoid and misanthropic about the dangers children face. Donald Findlater, director of research and development at the Lucy Faithfull Foundation, is quoted on the Home Office website warning:

> Sex offenders are mostly not the monsters commonly portrayed in the media – they are people we know, often people we care for … The police only know about known offenders, and if you have concerns about someone who

the police do not know, this does not mean they are automatically 'safe'. We should all remain vigilant to the warning signs so we can take action if necessary.[89]

Culturally, children are subject to a barrage of emotionally charged propaganda that hypes up fear of sexual abuse as a lifetime threat. A recent video created by aid agency CARE Norway called 'Dear Daddy', which has gone viral, highlights the trend.[90] The film starts as a letter from an unborn baby girl to her father, calling on men around the world 'to nip misogynist culture in the bud' by 'refusing to accept any kind of abuse towards women – whether physical or verbal, or even masquerading as a "joke"'. The unborn daughter narrator lists all of the possible – and horrific – things that could happen throughout her lifetime at the hands of men. By sixteen, she will have already been groped or pressured into sex by a boy while she is drunk; by twenty-one, she will

89 'Greater protection for children as sex offender disclosure scheme goes national', www.gov.uk, 27 March 2011

90 '#DearDaddy Rape Culture YouTube Video Gets 2.7 Million Views', *Inquisitr*, 16 December 2015

have been raped; and later in life, she seems to end up in an abusive relationship that puts her life at risk.

The 'Dear Daddy' protagonist asks, 'Am I over-reacting? I'm raised not to be the victim type.' Well, yes, she is over-reacting, or rather the adults who created the propaganda film are, and in doing so emphasise the cliché that young women are likely to be lifelong victims, while boys are stereotyped as a threat. This also fits a pattern: there seems to be a perverse relish in elevating danger, risk and threat when talking to young people about sexual abuse. The erstwhile adult role of reassuring the young and telling them not to over-react is replaced by grown-ups revelling in telling horror stories; if once when children had nightmares, we told them not to worry; now we tell them their nightmares are real life.

There is, of course, so much more to say on this issue, but suffice to conclude that one of society's obsessions over recent years has been *safeguarding* children. It might have begun as a noble aim, but it has in the event institutionalised a climate of distrust and fear that undoubtedly has been internalised by those who now demand safe spaces. Having grown up in an environment where their protection was the first priority, those children have become adults and are still demanding to be protected.

Blurring the line between physical and psychological harm

Today's offended students often show a marked degree of over-reaction to words that make them feel uncomfortable. They equate speech itself, and often the most innocuous comments, with physical violence. In this, they are simply extending how they were taught as children to respond disproportionately to damaging words. That's because the child protection narrative they have been raised on makes a particular feature of blurring the line between physical and psychological harm. For example, children's charities and NGOs constantly broaden definitions of abuse this way and, in doing so, actively encourage children to be suspicious of entirely harmless, informal, emotional interactions and tensions, even within their own families.

A few years ago, Action for Children lobbied heavily for an eye-catching 'Cinderella Law' that threatened prison to parents or carers for emotional abuse, something that included everything from 'ignoring a child's presence (to) failing to stimulate a child'. Thankfully, there was a backlash and the then Justice Minister Damian Green appeared to back off, although he still managed to add the slippery phrase 'psychological suffering' to existing law.

Already, from 2001 onwards, 'emotional abuse' has been a key part of civil law's definition of neglect and is regularly deployed when local authorities attempt to take children into care. The chair of the Local Government Association's Children and Young People Board, Councillor David Simmonds, boasts that 'emotional abuse is currently the second most common category of registration for children on a child protection plan, which indicates the extent to which social workers are already acting to protect children from this type of abuse'.[91]

That is shocking enough, but a quick glance at the promiscuous use of the term in local government literature

---

91 Quoted in 'Emotional abuse of children to become criminal offence', Children & Young People Now, 5 June 2014

suggests councils are coming close to inciting children to interpret every act of parental discipline as damaging. Moray Council advises youngsters that emotional abuse is when someone 'shouts down at you' or 'tries to control you or push you too hard' – in other words, a direct demonisation of legitimate parental admonishment. When the advice warns that it's abuse if your parents 'make you do things that are not your responsibility, like caring for your brothers and sisters', sibling babysitters may now interpret their treatment on a par with physical assault.

Harrow Council's list of psychological abuse includes 'being pressurised or manipulated into making decisions'. As all parents know, unless we manipulate or pressurise recalcitrant offspring, few would get up in the morning or go to school, let alone revise for exams. Meanwhile, North Lincolnshire Council says emotional abuse may include 'putting inappropriate expectations on a child that are over and above their capabilities and age' – otherwise known has having high aspirations for your child. As for 'not giving the child the opportunity to express their views, deliberately silencing them or "making fun" of what they say', well, hands up, I'm guilty, as is every parent who has told the kids to be quiet and get on with their homework.

The significance of this greater use of the notion of emotional abuse for this book's argument is how it provides official sanction for the idea that mere words can be harmful. In *On Liberty* John Stuart Mill allowed for 'one very simple principle' that allowed free speech to be limited: 'The only purpose for which power can be rightfully exercised over any member of a civilised community, against his will, is to prevent harm to others.'[92] Mill could not have anticipated the twenty-first century's therapeutic turn, whereby the harm principle would be broadened from the physical to the mental realm. But, as it is the case that 'psychological harm' and 'emotional abuse' are now part of a young person's vocabulary, they furnish today's easily offended with justifications to update Mill and explain that language and attitudinal assaults are as harmful as physical violence.

---

92 J. S. Mill, *On Liberty* (London: Longman, Roberts, & Green Co., 1869). Library of Economics and Liberty [Online], available from http://www. econlib.org/library/Mill/mlLbty1.html; accessed 11 March 2016

Culprits: the anti-bullying bandwagon

The bastard child of the child protection industry that has done most to inculcate children with the idea that speech causes long-term damage is the anti-bullying bandwagon. It has contributed enormously to frightening today's kids with stories of the threat posed by their peers, while also pathologising quite normal peer-to-peer tensions.

Anti-bullying has grown exponentially over the past twenty years. Under the School Standards and Framework Act 1998, state schools are required to have anti-bullying policies. New forms of bullying and powers to intervene are on the rise. The Education Act 2011 gives teachers stronger powers to tackle cyberbullying by providing a specific power to search for and delete inappropriate images or files on electronic devices and mobile phones. Government-backed bodies now provide special training in spotting sexist, sexual, homophobic and transphobic bullying.

In 2005, when he was the Children's Commissioner for England, Sir Al Aynsley-Green claimed that the one issue 'every child I have met has been affected by, with virtually

no exceptions, is bullying'.[93] But that should be no surprise when we look at how bullying is defined today.
Fifteen years ago, my ten-year-old niece came home in
tears and, after coaxing, told me that she was being bullied at school. Was she being beaten up by nasty older
kids? Having her dinner money stolen? Her head pushed
down the girls' toilet? Eventually she revealed that some
of her friends had gone to the cinema without her. I was
relieved and started to reassure her: this wasn't bullying,
we all fall out with friends and it is part of growing up, she
would find better friends etc. However, she indignantly
corrected me and quoted her school's anti-bullying policy on 'exclusion from friendship groups' and 'exclusion
at playtime or from social events and networks'.

My niece even seems to have neuroscience on her
side. Act Against Bullying, a campaigning charity, gives
a scientific explanation for why 'exclusion bullying' literally hurts: 'We have always known that being left out
of things on purpose can cause hurt but now science
is beginning to prove it. In fact the notion of feeling

---

93 'Schools "in denial" over bullying', BBC News, 13 November 2005

deliberately excluded causes the same sensation in a pain centre of the brain as an actual physical injury.'[94]

Helene Guldberg, whose book *Reclaiming Childhood: Freedom and Play in an Age of Fear* perceptively exposes so many of the problems with the obsession with bullying, notes how an industry of self-styled anti-bullying experts has increasingly expanded definitions of bullying into the psychological realm. Bullying now includes: 'teasing and name-calling'; 'having your stuff messed about with'; 'spreading rumours'; 'verbal sexual commentary'; 'homophobic taunting'; 'insensitive jokes'; 'bullying gestures'; and even just being 'ignored by other kids'.

Children are subjected to an endless stream of anti-bullying assemblies, activities, books, movies, specially written school dramas and, of course, celebrity victims. There seems barely a celebrity who has not publicly spoken out to support the anti-bullying movement. Tom Cruise, Ryan Gosling, Demi Lovato, Selena Gomez, Eminem, Christina Hendricks, Chris Rock, Justin

Timberlake, Ellen DeGeneres, Kelly Clarkson, David Guetta, Mika, Tyra Banks and Rihanna are just some of the celebrities who have declared that they, too, were victims of bullying. To some people, this parade of former victims who have gone on to considerable personal success might be evidence that being bullied need not have a long-term impact on someone's life chances. But this public endorsement of the bullied young person as someone who will gain maximum sympathy and adult attention inevitably encourages children to self-identify as 'bullied'. When the Children's Commissioner suggests a termly bullying questionnaire for every child, the outcome can only be to encourage children to examine all their everyday interactions through the prism of bullying.

Inevitably, this all eventually plays out in censorious classrooms, with a hyper-sensitive atmosphere that translates juvenile childish playground insults into serious matters of bullying. Any kid who wants to get a peer – or even a teacher – into trouble only needs shout 'bully' (especially if preceded by the epithet of 'racist', 'homophobic' or 'sexist' to add extra moral force), and the wrath of officialdom will descend.

Having been reared into a fear of bullying as children, we can hardly be surprised that such fears become a major preoccupation for that same generation when they grow up, whether on campus or in the workplace. So, predictably, microaggression advocates now claim that bullying is part of the same spectrum and continues into adulthood. Speaking not about children but grown-ups, one author describes 'microaggressive behaviours, such as … quieting opposing voices by purposely leaving them out of key discussions' or 'ensuring that their viewpoints prevail by not mentoring and nurturing the talent of those who come from diverse backgrounds'.[95]

Sapping resilience

Anti-bullying's contribution to creating our over-offended young adults involves its inculcation of a heightened sense of harm caused by words and an over-reaction to the rough and tumble of everyday life. But this is not just a threat to free speech. Dangerously, it seems to be sapping young

---

95 'Bullying & Microaggressions', *Psychology Today*, 23 January 2011

people's ability to cope with life. Even policy makers are beginning to worry about where this might lead in terms of the young lacking resilience. As Education Secretary, Nicky Morgan launched a £3.5 million grant scheme for character education, with the aim to instil 'grit' in pupils, including a rather misjudged initiative for schools to invite England squad rugby stars into the classroom because 'rugby teaches how to bounce back from setbacks'.

But such schemes are insignificant set next to the resources devoted to anti-bullying by the department and the ongoing suggestion that bullying, broadly defined, can be devastating. In November 2015, a Department for Education spokesman told *The Guardian*: 'We recognise the impact bullying can have on mental health and we are investing £1.4 billion over the next five years for young people's mental health services.'[96] This linking of bullying to mental illness and the idea that it causes 'life-long damage' really concerns me. I fear it is the anti-bullying industry that is the real threat to young people's

---

96 'Fewer school bullies but cyberbullying is on the increase', *The Guardian*, 16 November 2015

state of mind. Rather than reassure, it adamantly stresses, indeed exaggerates, the harmful effects of bullying. Such scaremongering is impacting on young people's coping mechanisms and possibly exacerbating the problem. As such, it actually contributes to the young feeling overly anxious, and ironically creates an atmosphere likely to encourage symptoms of mental ill health. The headline should be 'anti-bullying causes mental illness'.

The anti-bullying industry has made a virtue of catastrophising, always arguing things are getting worse. With the advent of social media, bullying experts are quick to point out there is now no escape: 'Bullying doesn't stop when school ends; it continues twenty-four hours a day.' Children's charities continually ratchet up the fear factor. Surely it is irresponsible when Sarah Brennan, CEO of YoungMinds, declares that if 'devastating and life-changing' bullying isn't dealt with 'it can lead to years of pain and suffering that go on long into adulthood'.[97]

---

97 'Serious mental health consequences for children and young adults as a result of bullying in schools – children, teachers and GPs call for more support', Press release for Anti-Bullying Week, November 2015, www.anti-bullyingalliance.org.uk

Maybe I am being over-cynical about the anti-bullying bandwagon, and there is a danger that such a critique will cause me to be labelled callous and hard-hearted. Certainly, when you read of some young people's heart-breaking experiences, there is no doubt that it can be a genuinely harrowing experience to go through. But when we hear these sad stories, surely our job as adults should be to help children and young people put these types of unpleasant experience behind them, to at least put them in perspective, rather than stoking up their anxieties and telling them they may face 'years of pain and suffering'.

Indeed, sensationalising the effects of bullying, and constantly emphasising how traumatic it is, can counter-productively make children over-react to events, sometimes with tragic consequences. Israel Kalman, creator of the American organisation Bullies2Buddies.com, an organisation that is critical of mainstream anti-bullying approaches, draws this out when discussing the controversial topic of bullycides (suicides allegedly prompted by bullying):

> Kids are taking their lives not because they are being
> attacked by violent gangs with knives and guns but

because they can't tolerate being insulted. And the schools, under the guidance of the bullying experts, are unwittingly encouraging kids to get upset by insults: they have replaced the ending of original 'sticks and stones' slogan with '...but words can scar me forever' and '...but words can kill me'. So when they get insulted, are they going to think, 'No big deal; it's only words'? No. They are going to think, 'Oh, no, I'm being insulted! Words can kill me!'[98]

Hopefully Kalman's grim predictions will not come true. But he has a point when he emphasises how anti-bullying campaigns constantly focus on young people's vulnerability and teach them that they need psychological 'support' in order to cope. This not only means children will see themselves as victims, it also chips away at their mental resilience. With this, combined with being endlessly told that the world is a fearful, abuse-riven place, that everyday experiences and emotional harm will cause them long-lasting damage (both to their bodies and their minds), is it any wonder that

---

98 'Blowing bullying out of all proportion', spiked, 27 June 2012

by the time they become young adults, they seem to be verging on genuine 'psychological collapse'? Preloaded with anxiety, they are ill-equipped to deal with a whole new set of grown-up challenges associated with leaving home and dealing with the expectations and responsibilities of maturity. So now Generation Snowflake goes off to college scared, over-protected, risk-averse and preoccupied by their well-being. What happens next should surprise no one.

Stressed-out students

Mental illness is said to have reached epidemic proportions in universities. A survey from the National Union of Students (November and December 2015), on behalf of the All Party Parliamentary Group on students, discovered that a staggering 80 per cent of respondents said they'd experienced mental health issues in the last year, a massive third admitting that they'd had suicidal thoughts. Interestingly, the numbers are rising alongside universities going to some lengths to cater for increasing mental health problems. Colleges are now awash with weekly therapy groups, courses such as 'Keeping Calm and in Control', 'Mindfulness for Depression' and 'Building Social Confidence', along with 'Anxiety 101' workshops. Some British universities are importing the American idea of Pet Therapy Days, noting that both Harvard Medical School and Yale Law School have 'resident therapy dogs in their libraries that can be borrowed through the card catalogue just like a book'.[99] For example, the University of Central Lancashire's student union organised its first 'puppy room' event in May 2015 as part of its SOS (Stressed Out Students) campaign. Universities even use their well-being services in PR marketing campaigns to attract new recruits.

Jennifer Cádiz, when deputy president of NUS Scotland, described the spiralling numbers of students seeking support for their mental health as 'a personal tragedy for thousands and a huge waste of talent'. But what seems more of a tragedy is the bleak view of university being sold to students by their own union. Cádiz

---

99 'For stressed college students, a doggone good way to relax', *USA Today*, 15 May 2012

says that many students 'begin university or college with the expectation of it being the "best years of your life"', but concludes that this hope is 'hugely misguided'.[100] Even trying to enjoy yourself at university is problematic. Aoife Inman, nineteen, a second-year student at the University of Manchester, was quoted by *The Guardian* as complaining that 'University was pitched to me as "the best years of your life" and there is definitely an anxiety among young people to live up to that expectation ... You can feel constant disappointment for not fitting the student stereotype.'[101]

It is tragic, too, that students now describe themselves as mentally ill when facing what are the routine demands of student life and independent living. The NUS survey reports that students' feelings of crippling mental distress are primarily course-related and due to academic pressure. In 2013, in response to that year's NUS mental health survey, an article cheerily entitled

---

100 'Silently Stressed report reveals soaring mental ill-health rates', NUS Scotland, 16 November 2010

101 'Majority of students experience mental health issues, says NUS survey', *The Guardian*, 14 December 2015

'Feeling worthless, hopeless … who'd be a university student in Britain?' listed one young writer's anxiety-inducing student woes that span the whole length of her course: 'Gruelling interview processes are not unusual, especially for courses like medicine, dentistry, and veterinary science, or for institutions like Oxbridge.' And then: 'Deadlines come thick and fast for first-year students, and for their final-year counterparts, the recession beckons.'[102] Effectively, the very requirements of just being a student are typified as inducing mental illness.

It can be hard to have sympathy with such youthful wimpishness. But I actually don't doubt the sincerity of these 'severe' symptoms experienced by stressed-out students. That is what is most worrying – they *really are* feeling over-anxious about minor inconveniences and quite proper academic pressure. Aoife Inman, the student quoted earlier, described the very act of leaving home as 'isolating' rather than exciting: 'Moving away from home and the securities of that environment means

---

102 Holly Baxter, 'Feeling worthless, hopeless … who'd be a university student in Britain?', *The Guardian*, 22 May 2013

that students are often left without a safety blanket if we begin to struggle.' No wonder that 22 per cent of the NUS survey blame 'symptoms' of homesickness for their mental ill health.

This all begins to feel very foreseeable. As we have seen, today's young adults have been cocooned, and schooled to view every problem in therapeutic terms. Dan Jones, director of counselling and psychological services at Appalachian State University in North Carolina, talks of today's students as being so used to 'extreme parental oversight' that they 'don't have the resilience of previous generations'. In consequence, 'many seem unable to steer themselves … They can't tolerate discomfort or having to struggle [and] don't have the ability to soothe themselves.'[103]

It is this inability to 'soothe themselves' which is of most concern. Of course, some of the challenges of student life can be stressful. Working all night to get that essay in, the periods of loneliness, being broke and living

---

103 Quoted by Lenore Skenazy, 'College Students Anxious Like Never Before: Why?', Free Range Kids, 1 June 2015

on lentils can take its toll. But pathologising these experiences just makes things a whole lot worse, suggesting there is no way to bounce back except via a medical professional. As Professor Frank Furedi notes: 'Distress is not an indicator of illness; it is an integral part of people's existence. When feeling distressed is medicalised, young people are prevented from developing their own ways of coping with painful experiences.'[104]

Yet, we have socialised children and young adults to think of themselves as weak and fragile, reared them to believe that name-calling can lead to mental illness, that without therapy they won't be able to deal with independence, criticism or exams. This process has enfeebled them. They really are suffering a crippling malady. But it is one constructed by older generations' policies. With no clear idea of how to resolve things, the way they are taking ownership of this situation is even more destructive: they are starting to pathologise politics.

---

104 Frank Furedi, 'Trigger warnings are educational suicide', spiked, 29 June 2015

Medicalising student politics

It is hardly surprising that today's students go on to apply the therapeutic concepts that they have been brought up on to their understanding of the political world. Ian Dunt, writing about attempts to ban Germaine Greer from various university campuses, explains how 'it started just like all the other travesties of this sort, with the dull thud of comparison between offence, psychological damage and warnings of disorder'.[105] Dunt points out that this has been the pattern for years now: 'Political disagreement has been increasingly equated with mental trauma in a university culture dominated by a form of therapy-style political discourse', complaining that 'student groups have proved very effective at framing their demands for censorship in the language of a "duty of care" from the university'.

And it's true. The language of psychiatry now trips off activists' tongues, becoming commonplace in political culture, and in particular in relation to free-speech

---

105 Ian Dunt, 'Feminist backlash against the censors shows tide turning in free speech debate', Politics.co.uk, 30 September 2015

controversies. Words such as 'trauma' are deployed promiscuously to emphasise the awfulness of more and more life events and the consequence of offence. 'Phobias' are in abundance in a range of social contexts, far beyond psychiatry's glossary of mental disorders. Now we have accusations of Islamophobia, transphobia, bi-phobia, whorephobia – all of which conveniently mean that you can write off views that you disagree with as the products of conditions that make rational argument pointless.

'Triggering', in particular, has moved seamlessly from the medical lexicon into campus speech. We may bemoan that student activists demand trigger warnings on great works of literature, but they have taken this straight from the mental health and well-being manual that is now educational orthodoxy, endorsed by government and the university hierarchy. When NUS lists the percentages of anxious students, it does so under the heading 'mental distress triggers'. This at least approximates the correct use of the term, and hints that the specific clinical use of the notion is more at home in mental illness discourse than academic life.

What is triggering? As mentioned earlier, delegates

at the 2015 NUS Women's Conference were sent an infamous tweet: 'Some delegates are requesting that we move to jazz hands rather than clapping as it's triggering anxiety.' The message nodded to how psychiatry acknowledges that certain traumatic events can be triggered by certain sounds. Cases of post-traumatic stress disorder (PTSD) were first documented during the First World War when soldiers developed shell shock as a result of the harrowing conditions in the trenches. Such ex-soldiers might well react with alarm when triggered by the sound of a car backfiring. What is more, in official mental health terms, the ideas of triggering someone with PTSD to 'relive traumatic events through flashbacks', emphasises that 'the person has experienced, witnessed, or been confronted with an event or events that involve actual or threatened death or serious injury, or a threat to the physical integrity of oneself or others, and his/her response involved intense fear, helplessness, or horror'. Compare this to NUS worries about clapping as a trigger, or the commentator who explained the policy by saying: 'It is worth acknowledging the omnipresence of anxiety as a factor in public meetings. We can all be made anxious by others around us – their exuberance, their laughter, their voices, can be "too much", particularly for those who are already vulnerable in one way or another.'[106]

It is depressing enough that young adults at a public meeting can equate their own social discomfort with the sort of trauma that a victim of war or torture might be justified in claiming. But now institutions are colluding with this, by accepting the medical category of trigger warnings into the fabric of educational life. Those academic departments that issue warnings about parts of courses so that students can avoid them, or put trigger warnings on texts, add another layer of legitimacy to the medicalised, vulnerable model of being a student.

Even schools are being embroiled in this quest to quarantine the young from the alleged triggering trauma of studying important intellectual works. In September 2015, AQA, the largest exam board in the UK, removed Émile Durkheim's seminal 1897 study of suicide from

---

106 Richard Seymour, 'The deadlock of identity essentialism', Lenin's Tomb, 26 March 2015

its A-level sociology syllabus. This work, so central to introducing pupils to sociological concepts, methods and statistics, was culled on the grounds that some students may be distressed by the topic. Rupert Sheard, AQA qualifications manager, explained that his organisation has a 'duty of care to all those students taking our course to make sure the content isn't going to cause them undue distress'. Refreshingly, Ged Flynn, Chief Executive of Papyrus, a charity working to prevent youth suicide, was disdainful about possible distress being used as a reason for changing the curriculum: 'It's been dropped because people feel uncomfortable teaching about suicide because of the stigma and pain. But suicide won't go away if we feel sensitive about it. Teachers need to get over themselves or get a new job.'[107]

But Flynn's down-to-earth common sense is not in vogue and it is the medicalising of the curriculum that seems to be the growing mainstream trend. Sadly, it is the young who will reap the negative consequences,

---

107 'Suicide dropped from sociology lessons – are some topics too sensitive for school?', *The Guardian*, 15 June 2015

in this instance with an impoverished education. In an article published last year by *Inside Higher Ed*, seven humanities professors wrote that the trigger-warning movement was 'already having a chilling effect on [their] teaching and pedagogy'. The American Association of University Professors reports that already the easiest way for faculty to stay out of trouble is to avoid material that might upset the most sensitive student in the class, noting: 'The presumption that students need to be protected rather than challenged in a classroom is at once infantilising and anti-intellectual.'

Infantilised and dependent

Increasingly we can see that one key result of a generation socialised into a safety-first culture is a generation unaccustomed to resolving problems informally or on their own. That is why today's students so often exhibit a sense of child-like dependence, a reliance on third parties. This is illustrated by the way the Yale students replied to Erika Christakis's Halloween email discussed at the start of this chapter: 'We were told to meet the offensive parties head on, without suggesting any modes or means to facilitate these discussions to promote understanding.' *The Atlantic*'s Conor Friedersdorf is suitably outraged at their pathetic immaturity:

> This beggars belief. Yale students told to talk to each other if they find a peer's costume offensive helplessly declares that they're unable to do so without an authority figure specifying 'any modes or means to facilitate these discussions', as if they're Martians unfamiliar with a concept as rudimentary as disagreeing in conversation, even as they publish an open letter that is, itself, a mode of facilitating discussion.

But this helplessness, students' admission that they're unable to facilitate discussions without authority figures to manage their conflicts, and their reliance on formal 'modes and means' to express grievance, is precisely the consequence of the institutionalised 'safety first' policies. All the trends that we have looked at so far foster dependence and, indeed, are antithetical to encouraging autonomy or free decision-making.

Take, for example, the way, in the name of anti-bullying initiatives, children are rarely left alone without the prying eyes of adults, their spontaneous interactions formalised into skills and codes of conduct. Their 'informal' activities are organised and supervised: playgrounds are re-designed to eliminate blind-spots for adult watchers; 'free time' is structured and monitored; dinner ladies are trained to spot behaviour deemed to be bullying and then report it through official channels. This adult intervention, littered with armies of learning mentors, behaviour improvement counsellors and anti-bullying buddies all anxiously poking around in children's spats, means we have abandoned a key tenet of socialisation: encouraging the young to be self-reliant, to develop their own nous, to grow up.

Perhaps the most intrusive, destructive and dependency-inducing trend of all is the way that the young are even denied the space to forge spontaneous friendships. When schools organise 'Good Friends Days', they dare to presume to teach friendship skills, with lessons in starting conversations, taking turns, developing empathy, being nice. There are best-practice friendship codes and checklists that schools display prominently, and even encourage pupils to recite by heart. The 'Developing Confidence' section of the educational resources website *Teaching Ideas* suggests introducing a 'feel-good box' into the classroom that involves every child writing something nice about another child each day. This is an entirely top-down initiative as the teacher 'tells each child who to write about, and then collects the notes afterwards'. Then there are workshops in 'how to show an interest in others' and to 'practise being persistent in asking to be included'.

Let alone the fact that enforced, compulsory friendships make a mockery of what friendship really means, by formalising and juridifying the informal areas of children's lives we are guaranteeing they grow up to become more reliant on outside intermediaries to fix their problems and even gain validation. The upshot of this is that we are draining the young's social and moral resources for handling certain situations informally and weakening their relationships with each other. No wonder today's students run to university bureaucrats and demand protection and bans; that today's NUS asks for compulsory consent classes to teach their members the appropriate way to conduct their most intimate sexual relationships.

That growing numbers of the young are labelled mentally ill leads to a particularly demoralising form of dependency, akin to a doctor/patient relationship. Seeing themselves as suffering illness means they can 'justify certain exemptions from normal expectations of performance' as sociologist Talcott Parsons puts it, because 'being ill cannot ordinarily be conceived to be the fault of the sick person'; we need to rely on the doctor, the therapist, outside agencies to make us better. By encouraging the young to wallow in a particular form of dependent victimhood associated with being sick, we let them off the hook and give them an excuse for avoiding the responsibilities of being grown up. This leads to expectations of a life spent being treated with kid gloves, being looked after; viewing (tea and) sympathy as a remedy; seeing support and protection as end goals.

But let me end this section with a paradox: while all of these trends that I have discussed privilege subjective feelings, they are the very antithesis of genuine human subjectivity. Historically and philosophically, being a subject requires sufficient autonomy to be able to act on the world. Today's overly subjective youth are instead reduced to the status of objects, acted upon by an overabundance of official bodies. However, a lack of awareness of this passivity can mean that young people themselves are flattered at such third-party interest. They seem to enjoy being mollycoddled, gaining an artificial sense of empowerment from their various victim roles as well as feeling legitimised as objects of institutional concern and interventions. Hence we have two seemingly contradictory phenomena: generational fragility combined with narcissistic self-belief in one's own importance.

ME, ME, ME: the entitled generation

If young people are wallowing in victimhood, how is it that there is also an acute generational sense of entitlement that borders on arrogance? It seems to be a contradiction. As someone who has been on the receiving end, there certainly seems little evidence of fragile wimpishness when you are being shouted down by those demanding you shut up and respect their safe space. Or ask Erika Christakis about timid students; since the Halloween email debacle, she has been forced to resign her teaching post.

In many of the offence disputes, the offended act as though they have not only the right to demand immediate apologies and climb-downs, but to dictate the very wording of those recantations; anything short of their version is met with further howls of rage. The offended expect to be listened to without challenge; dare disagree and you are accused of disrespect or privilege-checked. To quote one #RhodesMustFall supporter (tweeter Ebony_Thoughts), who reprimanded me for not cheering their demands, 'There is nothing to debate … this is not a matter of opinion, it's a matter of privilege.' They complain that they are being victimised if you don't validate their subjective, wounded feelings and respect their pain. Many have noted that they 'behave like bullies even as they see themselves as victims'. This was a noticeable feature of my 'Tale of two schools' at the start of this book.

Even supporters of safe spaces ('as a shield for

mutually supporting communities'), such as blogger Ken White, are concerned: 'Some use the concept of "safe spaces" as a sword, wielded to annex public spaces and demand that people within those spaces conform to their private norms. That's not freedom of association. That's rank thuggery, a sort of ideological manifest destiny.'[108]

This is vividly illustrated by recent events at the University of Missouri (aka Mizzou). Student activists forced the school's president Tim Wolfe to resign after demanding he 'admit to white privilege' and apologise for his alleged failure to address a series of racially tinged incidents; but they were not satisfied with *his* scalp and shortly after their victory turned on the press. 'We are calling the police because you aren't respecting us!' shouted one protester at a member of the media. Others chanted 'No comment!', holding placards saying: 'No Media, Safe Space' as they pushed and shoved reporters and cameramen. This no-comment approach

---

108 Ken White, 'Safe Spaces As Shield, Safe Spaces As Sword', Popehat, 9 November 2015

sums up an attitude that 'we're not answerable to any-one' from those who most persistently demand that others are silenced.

Subsequently, students at Smith College turned away journalists from their sit-in in support of the Mizzou activists unless they 'pledged allegiance to the cause'. Going against all principles of objective, unbiased jour-nalism, they demanded 'that any journalists or press that cover our story participate and articulate their solidar-ity with black students and students of colour ... By taking a neutral stance, journalists and media are being complacent in our fight.'[109]

Where and how did they gain such confidence, such self-belief in their own righteousness? One fascinating commentator on this issue, Jean M. Twenge, professor of psychology at San Diego State University, makes some compelling arguments about a generational 'epi-demic of narcissism'. She cites extensive evidence to note the apparent dichotomy of 'the current generation',

---

109 'Reporters barred from Smith College sit-in held in solidarity with Univer-sity of Missouri students unless they support movement', MassLive.com, 19 November 2015

who often lack coping skills and yet demonstrate 'both higher levels of assertiveness and confidence' than previous generations.[110]

Of course, as Twenge argues, 'people have always been self-absorbed during adolescence and young adulthood'. But why do today's young adults seem unable to go beyond this childish and adolescent narcissism, once understood as a natural developmental stage of growing up, but which now seems permanently fixed? Twenge quotes her co-author of *The Narcissism Epidemic: Living in the Age of Entitlement*, psychology professor W. Keith Campbell, to offer some explanations:

> People have always said young people are self-absorbed. They are. The difference is that cultures used to have rites to transform young people into adults, like male circumcision or walkabouts. Today, if you're twenty-eight years old and living in your Mom's basement eating Ho Hos and playing Xbox you will be called an 'emerging adult'.

---

110 Jean M. Twenge, 'Have young people always been self-absorbed?', The Narcissism Epidemic blog, 2 August 2010

Twenge agrees, saying: 'Our current culture does not require young men and women to "grow out" of their self-absorption for a very long time.'

There is a lot in this. After all, we live in a culture where colouring books have become a serious pastime for adults. But I think that the rot starts much younger. The corrosive attitudes that encourage narcissistic entitlement have been inculcated at a much earlier age, alongside the risk aversion already looked at. In Britain, journalist and former teacher Harry Mount says, 'Universities are reaping the whirlwind of two decades of child-centred education' and a 'lifetime of people saying "yes" … of never being told off'. He notes it is wrong to blame what he dubs 'the student emperors' for all this, saying the fault lies with 'the generation above – the teachers and parents who have so indulged them'.[111] Similarly, educational writer and teacher Martin Robinson asks how these self-appointed, thought-denying young aristos 'begin to believe they have the right

---

111 Harry Mount, 'It's time to say No to our pampered student emperors', *Daily Telegraph*, 29 December 2015

to rise above others?' Why are they so sure they have 'more noble thoughts than the rest', that they have the right 'to close down the thoughts and uttering' of others by issuing 'edicts from their moral high ground'? He concludes: 'They are not born, they are made, and one of the places that forges the new aristocracy is the school classroom.'[112]

I agree with Mount and Robinson that schools are culprits here. So, let's look at what particular features of schooling have created our ME, ME, ME 'student emperors'. The main two culprits I want to name and shame are the student voice movement and self-esteem advocates.

Culprit: student voice

A number of commentators have noted that one of the reasons that university authorities back down in offence disputes is 'partly to do with the changed relationship

---

112 Martin Robinson, 'A Classroom Should not be a Safe Space', Trivium21c blog, 30 November 2015

between students and the institutions they study in. Fees turned what was once a teacher–pupil relationship into a service–consumer one.'[113] This is an important point and it is undoubtedly true that fee-paying students have a greater sense of entitlement, being endlessly cajoled and flattered by institutions desperate to attract and retain undergraduates in a highly competitive market. The Student Voice Movement, when it plays out at university, can often involve litigious threats about customer dissatisfaction. Indeed, higher education institutions are as obsessed with courting students' approval, so that they score highly in official student satisfaction surveys, as they are with doing well in the Research Assessment Exercise. Keeping students satisfied feeds the sense that universities should centre on students' wishes and well-being often to the detriment of academic excellence.[114]

However, the prevalence of student voice is not simply

---

113 Ian Dunt, 'Feminist backlash against the censors shows tide turning in free speech debate', Politics.co.uk, 30 September 2015

114 Dr Joanna Williams looks at all aspects of this trend in *Consuming Higher Education: Why Learning Can't be Bought* (Bloomsbury Academic, 2012)

a consequence of students 'buying' their degrees. It starts in state schools, where it is more clearly an ideological assault on adult authority, and is driven by those who advocate that education should be pupil-centred. Harry Mount notes, in relation to the row over Rhodes's statue, that 'every time the authorities are accused of racism, they bend over backwards to soothe the offended egos of the little, tinpot dictators – rather than telling them that they, the teachers, are there to tell the students what to do; and not the other way round'. But asserting that lecturers know more than students, or teachers know more than pupils, jars with contemporary educational theory and practice that well and truly puts the young in the driving seat. One key mechanism for this is the increasingly prominent school 'Student Voice' movement.

Myriad Student Voice campaigns, charities and training schemes now champion a wide range of initiatives said to facilitate pupils' empowerment. Schools are told to 'put the learner firmly at the centre … [to make them] actively involved in every aspect of their own learning', and to 'consult and involve pupils when revising curriculum structures'. Encouraging learners to express their views about curriculum choices and 'in the provision of their own education' is considered best practice in improving classroom motivation, and is paraded as an example of Pupil Voice in action.

Of course, we shouldn't silence student voices as such; every teacher listens to the ceaseless ideas and chatter of hundreds of pupils every day. But institutionalised student voice can only create a misplaced sense of entitlement in pupils that confuses roles in the classroom, putting teachers on the defensive. And when Student Voice, a Phoenix Education Trust-backed campaign, demands that equal weight be given to 'the views of *the most important stakeholders in our education system –* the students (my emphasis)', one has to conclude that this can only undermine teachers' authority. And we should note that this authority is not some outdated, hierarchical attitude to the young, seeking to impose a Victorian 'seen but not heard' rule on pupils. Rather, it is recognition that teaching involves an unequal relationship, the conscious and regular imposition of pedagogic priorities on pupils regardless of their spontaneous inclinations, presupposing that the older generation has something valuable to impart to the young.[115]

But such a view of authority is considered hopelessly elitist and old-fashioned by many in the educational establishment. Now Student Councils are involved in everything from carrying out official observations of teachers to shadowing senior staff; pupil representatives are given official encouragement to assess the standard of lessons by OFSTED and sit on interview panels for school staff. Martin Robinson notes that any teacher 'who has faced the ignominy of being "interviewed" by a panel of fourteen-year-olds understands that pupil power is taken very seriously by some schools'.

This topsy-turvy approach, on a par with 'the lunatics taking over the asylum', undermines teachers' confidence. No wonder that, in the *TES*'s comprehensive 'collection of teaching resources to support pupil voice and school councils', one of the most popular sections is that seeking advice by teachers 'about

---

115 Claire Fox, 'Why student voice has gone way too far', *TES* magazine, 18 October 2013

to be interviewed for a new job by a school council or other group of students'. It is noted this can be daunting to prepare for, to such an extent that one job-seeker notes: 'I've got an interview and the first part is with the school council and I'm more nervous about that than the actual interview!'

No doubt few appointments are based solely on pupils' feedback. Robinson observes that, in reality, student voice is not a decisive feature in real decisions, 'it's window dressing, a sop, but it is part of the idea that what students say matters, as long as what they say doesn't rock the boat'. This possibly underestimates the worrying consequences of an approach that gives pupils' unchallenged opinions a sense of privilege. Even if it is window dressing, telling pupils that they are in any way responsible for getting a new teacher his/her salary allows pupils to arrogantly assume that 'we put you where you are'. And such practices can hardly encourage pupils to understand that teachers' suitability should be their experience and subject knowledge, the very expertise in which their authority derives, but which pupils are ill-equipped to assess.

Culprit: self-esteem

The demand that adults listen to children is also a key feature of the pernicious self-esteem movement, which stalks classroom practice. The US based National Association of School Psychologists published an influential paper on how parents and schools can boost self-esteem in children, and emphasised listening to children as core: 'Adults must listen carefully to the child without interrupting, and should not tell the child how to feel. They should avoid responses such as "Oh, that's silly to feel sad about not being invited to your friend's birthday party. You'll get over it."'[116] Meanwhile, the UK charity Family Lives tells parents they can help their children to build self-esteem by trying 'not to label, criticise or blame your child, as this would give them negative messages which can stick and can have a detrimental impact on their emotional well-being later on in life'.[117]

Is it any wonder that when a parent shouts at their

---

116 Ellie L. Young and Laura L. Hoffmann, 'Self-esteem in Children: strategies for parents and educators', The National Association of School Psychologists, 2004

117 Helping your child build self-esteem, www.familylives.org.uk

child for misbehaving, they can expect a hectoring lecture from their offspring about the importance of encouragement not reprimand, negotiation not negativity, all straight from the latest self-esteem manual they've been drilled in at school? This, combined with their exposure to the public health risk aversion already discussed, means it's impossible to have a fried breakfast with a nine-year-old without a lecture about the dangers of fatty foods. And who dares light a cigarette or sip a second glass of wine in their presence? Finger-wagging, know-it-all kids are very much the devil's spawn of self-esteem society.

One of David Cameron's many wheezes for restoring adult authority, announced in January 2016, was to suggest that we 'make it normal – even aspirational – to attend parenting classes' to learn how to discipline our children. This can only make things worse. When the state sends their parents back to school to learn child-rearing from 'experts', children will be further encouraged to conclude that their parents' authority is on shaky ground.

No wonder these same children grow up with an assumption that those in authority are weak and hopeless, that their own insights are at least on a par, that their voices are those that should be listened to. But it's a con, at children's expense. When self-esteem advocates tell us to flatter the young about their views, in reality they ask adults to abandon the difficult task of disciplining them. Emphasising that adults must 'express unconditional positive regard and acceptance for children' effectively destroys the intergenerational duty of passing on knowledge, setting boundaries for behaviour and the broader task of socialisation. It is not good for children and can mean adults indulging even the most destructive aspects of young people's behaviour. In 2013, a self-harming pupil at Unsted Park School in Godalming, Surrey was given a disposable safety razor to slash himself with, supervised by a teacher. A spokeswoman from selfharm.co.uk justified this irresponsible collapse of adult judgement using the mantras of pupil voice and self-esteem: 'The best way to help is to listen without judging, accept that the recovery process may take a while and avoid "taking away" the self-harm' because 'self-harm can be about control, so it's important that the young person in the centre feels in control of the steps taken to help them'.[118]

That's an extreme case but it touches on how focusing on the schoolchild's self-esteem can create the impression that the world should circle around pupils' desires. This in turn puts pressure on adults to tip-toe around young people's sensitivities and to accede to their opinions. Combined with student voice orthodoxies, this can lead to the peculiar diktat that teachers express respect for pupils' views, however childish or even poisonous.

For example, after the November 2015 massacre of Parisian revellers, I wrote an article for the *TES* explaining my fear that some teachers are tempted to adapt to the increasing passive support for jihadi identity politics evident among pupils. This is especially true in parts of France. One French teacher recalled a student who had refused keep the one minute's silence for the *Hebdo* victims by saying, 'I'm *not* Charlie; I think the terrorists did the right thing.' The teacher's response was telling:

---

118 'Self-harm pupil given razor at Unsted Park School', BBC News, 26 March 2013

'Children have the right to say silly things, to even say offensive things.' That's true. This is a book defending that right. But arguing for free speech and political tolerance is not an excuse for this sort of cultural cringe in the face of abhorrent ideas. We need to confront pupils who say stupid things, yet too often these sorts of views are indulged: 'So you favour a Caliphate and think 9/11 is a Zionist plot? That's an interesting idea. Any other views?'[119]

Gregg Henriques writes perceptively about a related phenomenon: the impact of telling parents, friends, coaches, therapists and educators that they must 'work hard to protect and enhance the self-esteem of our children'. He argues that the flip side of 'protect[ing] them from feeling badly about themselves' is that adults end up being overly 'careful about being too critical, or having them feel like they are lesser compared to their peers'. This can lead to over-indulgent 'helicopter' and 'snowplow' parents and 'teachers giving stickers and cupcakes for normal appropriate behavior, coaches giving trophies

---

119 Claire Fox, 'Don't just cringe – stand up to jihadi ideas', *TES* magazine, 18 December 2015

for kids showing up and all sorts of other well-meaning but deeply misguided attempts to protect children from negative feelings and experiences'.[120]

Unfortunately, as a consequence of such coddling, children never learn to cope with disappointment or accept criticism, essential skills that they will need as they grow up. Henriques explains:

> Effective functioning involves … learning to cope with normal stress and distress without becoming overwhelmed. This means that kids need to build up what I call emotional calluses. Disappointment, stress and frustration are all normal parts of everyday living. They are fine and essential to experience … There are bumps in the road and the failures and minor injuries to pride keep us honest and authentic. That is life."[121]

Self-esteem is no fringe, progressive educational quirk.

---

120 Gregg Henriques, 'What is Causing the College Student Mental Health Crisis?', *Psychology Today* Theory of Knowledge blog, 21 February 2014

121 Gregg Henriques, 'Self-Esteem Nation', *Psychology Today* Theory of Knowledge blog, 23 November 2013

As professor of sociology Frank Furedi says in his 2003 book *Therapy Culture: Cultivating Vulnerability in an Uncertain Age*, an emphasis on the message that 'you are what you feel about yourself' rather than on the basis of real achievements in society 'is an all-powerful contemporary notion that has gripped popular culture'. Nowadays, the use of the term self-esteem, and its accompanying emphasis of privileging of the self, is mainstream enough to be a go-to word for everyone from TV personalities to politicians. In December 2015, a new mental health charity aptly called 'The Self-Esteem Team' (who 'travel the UK going into schools to teach students on mental health, body image and self-esteem') signed up high-profile popular culture figures to launch its #NewYearsReVolution. The likes of *Geordie Shore*'s Charlotte Crosby, *Countdown*'s Rachel Riley and fitness model and prolific Instagrammer Michelle Lewin (who has 6.9 million followers) featured in a film promoting well-being.[122]

---

122 'Charlotte Crosby reveals her New Year resolution is to spend LESS time on her phone in video that urges women to "focus on yourself, not your selfie" in 2016', Mail Online, 31 December 2015

The campaign's slogan – 'Here's to the new you, working on your self, not just your selfie' – was clever enough, but emphasised how self-esteem is now used to convey the idea that YOU are fine just as you are, with a rather unsavoury emphasis on self-love, arguably far more malevolent than any selfie craze. One of the Self-Esteem Team organisers, Nadia Mendoza, wrote in *The Independent*, 'Having high self-esteem and respecting the house it lives in (YOU) is like buying a car then keeping it shiny because you like it. You wouldn't just leave it to fester and fall apart. In a nutshell, *love the skin you're in…*'[123]

'Loving the skin you're in' is a consistent message spouted by self-esteem advocates. Everything from self-help guides to teen magazines regularly feature tips on 'being your own best friend' and 'reaffirming your self-worth'. Advice includes such gems as writing down 'amazing things about yourself every morning'. So if we wonder where Generation Snowflake gets

---

123 '#NewYearsReVolution: Jamal Edwards and Rachel Riley join the Self-Esteem Team campaign to rethink resolutions', *The Independent*, 30 December 2015

its sense of self-regard from, the self-esteem move-ment must take some of the credit (or blame). It is an industry dedicated to creating ego-boosting, self-orientated youth.

Another self-esteem trope is not to have any truck with criticism from others. Mendoza tells us her self-esteem-related New Year's resolution is: 'To not worry about the haters, because their opinions don't define me and their judgement says more about them than it does about me.' But this suggests ignoring criticism, whether valid or not, as a matter of principle. Indeed, those who criticise you are actually blamed for creat-ing your low self-esteem in the first place. Bustle.com writer Brianna Wiest tells readers that a lack of self-esteem begins 'when your emotions weren't validated as a child'. This is because '[w]hen someone told you what you thought, how you felt, or what you did was wrong, you began to believe that you needed to consult someone or something else to tell you what is "right"'. Her recommendation for boosting self-esteem is that you 'remind yourself that what you feel is valid, who you are is worthy, and that the only problem you have is not being able to accept the way you are. (Nothing more, nothing less)'.[124]

'Accept the way you are: Nothing more, nothing less' is a recipe for conservative complacency. It also feeds into creating today's offence generation whose recipe for any discomfort is to set up a safe space and surround themselves with those who will agree with them and endorse their viewpoint. It additionally encourages a tangible sense of stasis that implies that we all know everything we need to know; we have no need to be taught new ideas, we just need to express ourselves. This is reflected in, and encouraged by, debates on pupil-centred school curricula, with pupils regularly told that what they are taught is all about 'YOU'.

It's all about YOU, YOU, YOU

Just three days after the Paris terror attacks in November 2015, a bizarre school lesson plan called 'ISIS – a

---

124 Brianna Wiest, '7 Mantras For When You Need To Boost Your Self-Esteem', Bustle, 30 December 2015

theological problem' was uploaded to a popular class-room resources website purporting to help pupils 'understand' the terror group. What did this officially sanctioned lesson plan think would aid understanding? It asked fourteen- to sixteen-year-olds to imagine the world 'from the point of view of a soldier of faith' and suggested that they 'give three good reasons for joining Islamic State'. What? Who on earth were the 200 British teachers who thought it a good idea to download this lesson, with its suggested handout including reprinted sections from an IS propaganda magazine about holy war and 'fighting the barbaric Jews'?[125] Is there such a lack of faith in objectivity that it is assumed that young people can only grasp an understanding of radical jihad-ists by adopting their identity?

This particular example might be glaringly problem-atic, but it is a broader phenomenon unrelated to the specific thorny issue of how to tackle Islamic extremism in classrooms. Many curriculum initiatives over the last

---

125 'Outcry over lessons in "reasons for joining ISIS"', *Daily Mail*, 19 November 2015

decade focus on 'experiential learning' – the kids have to experience it in order to get it. In a National Union of Teachers (NUT) pamphlet, *Valuing Teachers, Valuing Education*, sent to all schools in late November 2015, the discussion of knowledge transmission was afforded little importance in contrast to the need to 'allow pupils to recognise themselves and their identities'.

Finding devices to 'allow pupils to recognise themselves' explains a popular pedagogic approach today that asks young people to cut and paste themselves into characters' shoes as an aid to understanding (hence, put yourself in the shoes of an ISIS 'soldier of faith'). This assumes pupils won't be interested unless they make the story about 'me me me', *literally* play-act identify with the dramatis personae of history, literature, art etc. So we have the art website vangoyourself.com aimed at engaging hard-to-reach young audiences. 'Vango' ('a jokey reference to Vincent Van Gogh', according to founder Jane Finnis) urges people to post 'selfies' of themselves and friends posing to look like Old Master paintings. Do Old Masters really need improving? Will teenagers really miss the beauty and genius of Botticelli or Picasso unless they make them relevant by plonking themselves into the middle of *The Birth of Venus* or *Guernica*? A similar initiative, the popular English literature app To Be Or Not To Be, asks 'readers' to 'choose your own adventure version of *Hamlet*'. One enthusiastic reviewer in *The Bookseller* explains: 'Maybe read the story first in the role of Ophelia and then Hamlet senior ... excellent entertainment.' The supposed novelty of being able to 'think yourself in protagonists' shoes' surely misses the point: this is just a shallow version of precisely what literature does so sublimely.

The aim of To Be Or Not To Be, as with other similar 'literacy' tools, is to put pupils centre-stage, suggesting to young readers that the aim of fiction should be to focus on *them*, rather than allowing the literature to take them away from themselves, to new, unknown worlds of imagination. At the very least this misunderstands the way we might conceive of ourselves in great works of literature. Even at its most intimate, when art seems to speak to us directly, it is by allowing us to transcend our own immediate experience. We realise we are not alone, but part of a human history. As inspirational teacher Hector explains in Alan Bennett's play *The History Boys*:

> The best moments in reading are when you come across
> something – a thought, a feeling, a way of looking at
> things – which you had thought special and particular
> to you. And now, here it is, set down by someone else,
> a person you have never met, someone even who is long
> dead. And it is as if a hand has come out, and taken yours.

Instead of Hector's universalist, timeless approach, we have today a relativist educational agenda that pushes updating the curriculum to make it relevant for today's pupils; to adapt Matthew Arnold's 'the best that has been thought and known' to accommodate the immediate thoughts and knowledge of today's pupils. In 2013, objecting to Michael Gove's changes to the history GCSE curriculum, which shifted emphasis, a motion at the NUT conference complained that because 'little account is taken of children's potential interests … experience, lives … the learner [is] … completely absent' from course content. This, the motion concluded, was 'sure to put them off the subject'.[126] The main lesson that pupils would learn from these teachers' views is that they, rather than acquiring knowledge, are all that matters.

Educating the young traditionally allowed new generations to join in the Great Conversation of civilisation by furnishing access to the works and insights of previous generations of thinkers and writers from the dawn of history. Today it seems we only want to facilitate a conversation in which the young talk to themselves, about themselves.

Treating the curriculum as a mirror in this way inevitably gives pupils a sense that they are the centre of the universe. This is our mini-me Generation Snowflakers being told that thousands of years of literature, philosophy and historical insight should be sidelined to accommodate to their immediate interests. This inevitably feeds the idea that their own identity should be a trump card.

The *New York Times* called 2015 'the year we obsessed over identity' and we have already discussed in Part I

---

126 Claire Fox, 'Face the facts: without them we know nothing', *TES*, 26 April 2013

how the raging, internecine culture wars surrounding politicised identity are a major factor in today's free-speech disputes. Imagine how dangerous it is to combine this destructive trend with an educational policy that socialises the young into believing their very identity as 'yoof' deserves a special sort of recognition. This is precisely what we do when schools' policy takes that old feminist slogan 'the personal is political' to its most logical, narcissistic conclusion and turns each individual pupil into her own self-regarding, individual, 'Me Me Me' identity group. One small step to the dreaded words – 'As Me, Me, Me I find that offensive…'

To recap: we – adult society – have scared the young by 'catastrophising' an endless list of existential fears, made them over-anxious about their own bodies and abuse from adults and peers, have elided abusive words with physical violence, medicalised the perfectly natural upsets of growing up, and created a knee-jerk assumption that they need to be protected in order to be safe. At the same time, we have shielded them from criticism, suspended our critical judgement to massage their self-esteem, privileged and fawned over their student voice (at the expense of our own adult authority), and adapted education around their desires and interests.

We have, in short, created our own over-anxious but arrogant, easily-offended but entitled, censoriously thin-skinned Frankenstein monster: Generation Snowflake.

Now it's time to address our creature directly…

Part III

Letter to a generation

It's time to talk to, and argue with, Generation Snowflake – and their opponents

I REGRET TO SAY *that the shenanigans on campus mean the current generation of students is becoming a laughing stock. They have been labelled as little emperors, tinpot dictators, Stepford students, and have even merited special lampooning in a* South Park *episode dedicated to Safe Space. This is an appeal for those students to take a step back and wise up.*

So, here are a few thoughts for Generation Snowflake,

but I also want to talk to their critical peers, the Anti-Snowflakers, who are rightly fed up of being tarred with the same brush, tainted with the thin-skinned label and demonised as bullies for daring to stand up to the easily offended. In this chapter, I will speak to both groups separately and then as one, to argue that it is time to create something more positive and robust than today's offence wars: a critical climate that really is in opposition to some of the more destructive social and cultural trends that this generation has come to exemplify.

Dear Generation Snowflake,

I know you like to present yourselves as rebels, kicking against the 'establishment' pricks, but one of the striking things about your contemporary youthful rebellion is its startling lack of rebelliousness. In many instances, your campaigns to silence offence, to demand safety above freedom, are no real challenge to the authorities, who have historically been quick to ban people for their own reasons without any help from students. Don't be fooled into thinking you have the old authorities on the run. Haven't you noticed that they already agree with your prejudices? Perhaps the reason you are so successful in getting publications banned, statues culled, and fatwas declared on unpalatable views is that you are ventriloquising the orthodox opinion that you think you are rebelling against, even acting as patsies for the establishment.

Helen Lewis of the *New Statesman* argues that you are 'rebelling against [your] parents' generation and its liberal deification of free speech'.[127] This over-flatters you, and them. There may be an appearance of rebelling, but actually there is nothing you offer that offends the preoccupations of your parents' generation; indeed, you tend to mouth the very same concerns that they reared you on, using language and concepts that you have been taught at school. It is time to realise that you are simply ciphers for a previous generation's anxieties. Your rebellion is pretty shallow; you are kicking an open door.

---

127 Helen Lewis, 'What the row over banning Germaine Greer is really about', *New Statesman*, 27 October 2016

You talk as though you are at the vanguard of new insights into gender, race and equality and that free speech has a responsibility to defend diversity and promote social justice. Perhaps – unaware of your lack of originality – you don't realise that you are often simply mouthing the multiculturalist, identity-laden values that PC Baby Boomers and academic cultural relativists have been pushing at you for years (even if you sometimes take these ideas to absurd illogical conclusions, using new jargon).

Tell me, is it a victory for student power when a Conservative minister orders university vice-chancellors to set up a task force to deal with the sexist 'lad culture' on campus? When the business secretary, Sajid Javid, demands college authorities bring about 'cultural change' to protect female students from groping and 'inappropriate touching', is it really a win for feminist activists? Or should you remember that this is the same political class that has propagated decades of fears about sexual abuse, as discussed in Part II? They have simply adapted their worries about safeguarding children into a language palatable for NUS bureaucrats and student feminist campaigners.

Another example is the campaign to remove the 'offensive' statue of nineteenth-century colonialist Cecil Rhodes from Oriel College, Oxford. You assume that such campaigns are your generation's version of Gramsci's 'long march through the institutions'. Oxford international relations student Sizwe Mpofu-Walsh, speaking as a representative of the #RhodesMustFall campaign on BBC Radio 4's *Today*, boasted: 'We think that Oxford is institutionally racist … we are forcing the university to confront the problem and probably doing a better job of it than any generation before us.' He was blasting university chancellor Lord Chris Patten's admirable but woefully belated attempt to hold firm.[128]

Oriel donors finally put their foot down and refused to remove the statue but, even so, posing this as a generational fight against the old guard is misplaced. The college's upper echelons had already given much ground. Oriel's governors' prevarication indicates that they were infected by cultural revolution-style self-loathing about

---

128 Interview with Sarah Montague, *Today*, BBC Radio 4, 14 January 2016

their 'hideously white' heritage. So, instead of telling you to grow up, sod off and realise that airbrushing history is not the way smart young people should react to complicated events from the past, the college bent over backwards to reassure you that they broadly agreed with your historical illiteracy. Instead of firmly reminding you that it is anachronistic to apply 21st-century value judgements to nineteenth-century colonialism, Oriel management, embarrassed by its own institution's un-PC historic roots, rushed to announce it would erect a sign below the statue to show that 'the College does not in any way condone or glorify [Rhodes's] views or actions', while taking down a Rhodes plaque on the wall of another college. It then launched that now obligatory evasion of leadership – 'a structured six-month listening exercise'[129]– which it eventually had to abandon due to pressure from financial donors.

Inevitably, you – the protestors – are up in arms that the college reneged on the 'listening exercise': 'Why

---

129 'Statement by Oriel College about the issues raised by the Rhodes Must Fall in Oxford petition', Oriel College website, 17 December 2015

did they listen to donors, and not us? It's not fair.'[130] Your disbelief is hardly surprising given that you have been reared in an era of Student Voice, your opinions appeased and fawned over (as discussed in Part II). But before whining too much, it's worth asking yourselves why every institution has a youth advisory board, indulges in youth consultations, employs youth ambassadors? Aren't you a teeny bit suspicious that those in authority are constantly asking you for your opinions? Please don't be flattered into imagining it is your views *per se* that they are listening to. This is just part of a trend whereby those in authority abdicate responsibility by outsourcing decision-making to the young. More often than not, *you* are being asked to say what *they* want to say, but in a more youthful, credible way.

Let me give you an example of how this can mean cynically using 'young voices' to dub over an existing policy. I was once asked to debate the head of education at a major local authority on whether citizenship

---

130 'Uproar over decision to keep Cecil Rhodes statue at Oxford College', *Daily Telegraph*, 29 January 2016

should be a compulsory subject in the school curriculum. In the event, my eminent opponent, one of the chief architects of citizenship education, deferred his speech to a group of local pupils, arguing that their views were more important than anything he could say. So out trotted five eleven- and twelve-year-olds to read out a series of statements about how important citizenship classes would be for their future. They received a standing ovation, although perhaps less for what they said than that it was they – as representatives of the voice of youth – who said it. How could I stick the boot in to these innocent, earnest 'tweens' and tell them they were talking rubbish? How could I tell them that they were too young to understand the implications of curriculum change without looking like a heartless brute? I did, but I had been set up – and, more importantly, so had they.

Of course, you are not so easily manipulated. Or so you like to think. However, in many of today's free-speech conflicts, protesters are simply allowing the authorities to enact their own enfeebled agenda through you. For example, in the US, when masters of Harvard

PART III

University's undergraduate residential houses unanimously agreed to abolish the title of 'house master' after student complaints that the word 'master' carries connotations of slavery, you may think this is 'another historic victory for our enlightened generation'. Maybe not. Actually, these same house masters had been discussing abolishing their own official name long before student protests. Harvard's Dean, Rakesh Khurana, admitted that 'for some time' he had 'not felt comfortable personally with the title'. Indeed, in this and many instances, it is often those who run institutions who are calling the shots, sanitising linguistics and cleansing history. Khurana argued that he recognised the difficulty of the 'social meaning' of the term 'master', explaining that his recommendation to change the title had been 'rooted in a broad effort to ensure that the college's rhetoric, expectations, and practices around our historically unique roles reflect and serve the 21st-century needs of residential student life'.[131] So we are back to those safe homes again, cleansed of any discomforting words, but this time

131 'Q&A on changing house master title', *Harvard Gazette*, 6 December 2015

materialising as a top-down impulse, with a stage army of students believing that they are in the driving seat.

Back in the UK, you might think that it's a generational victory that Cambridge University has been forced to take down its 'Dear World ... Yours, Cambridge' fundraising video. The film, produced to raise £2 billion, was removed from public view on YouTube in response to nothing more than a letter of protest. The offence in this instance was that the video was fronted by the historian and Fitzwilliam College alumnus David Starkey, who protesters claimed was 'aggressively racist', citing a BBC *Newsnight* programme on the riots in 2011. Starkey was denounced as the 'wrong face' to represent a commitment to diversity because of his white man 'confidence'. According to student Lola Olufemi, 'What is particularly harrowing about Starkey is the confidence with which he was able to air such opinions. Such is the confidence of white men...'[132]

Never mind Starkey's confidence, perhaps you should

---

132 Lola Olufemi, The David Starkey problem with our publicity', *Varsity*, 2 November 2015

be more worried about the lack of confidence exhibited by his fellow academic critics in the very role of a university lecturer and its curriculum. Lucy Allen, a medievalist at Cambridge's English faculty, writing as her alter ego 'Jeanne de Montbaston', was happy to censor the 'Dear World' video because it 'perpetuates an image of educational hierarchy, with Starkey pinning us with his gaze, breathing professorial authority, speaking sonorous RP'. What she found offensive was the portrayal of 'a classic classroom scene' featuring 'teaching, for goodness' sake, using a chalk blackboard, like a relic of the good old days'. Goodness, a lecturer having the temerity to lecture! Starkey had obviously missed the memo from today's academic rule book that demands lecturers should be co-learners, a 'guide at the side' rather than a 'sage on the stage', to quote the mantra of all hip, anti-traditionalist educators. So before congratulating yourselves for pulling down arrogant academics from their pedestals, remember they are keen to dethrone themselves.

What Starkey says outside of academia on television seems less offensive than what his antagonists say inside

academia in seminars. Dr Allen, aka Ms de Montbaston, used the whole affair to discuss her anti-literary,
politicised approach to teaching on her Middle English romance course. She seems less concerned about
Starkey's alleged racism and more about the way 'popular medieval fictions generate and perpetuate bigoted
stereotypes – misogynistic, racist, disablist, xenopho-
bic and Islamophobic ... tired old images of blackness
and Judaism ... foreign "Others" and violent invaders'.
Her lectures critique 'Europe's medieval culture' for its
'rape myths and victim-blaming and ... tropes of the Bad
Mother and the deviant sexualised woman'.[133] Elsewhere,
Sarah Pett, a lecturer sympathetic to the #RhodesMust-
Fall campaign, complains that in eight years of university
teaching in the United Kingdom and South Africa, 'dead
white men rule the roost at ... universities ... [they] clog
up reading lists and dominate the syllabus, particularly
in subjects like philosophy and English literature'. She
argues the need 'to push dead white men like William

---

133 Jeanne de Montbaston, '"Dear World": David Starkey does not speak for
   Cambridge University on Race or Gender', Reading Medieval Books blog,
   12 November 2015

Shakespeare out of the limelight', complaining that the likes of 'Malory … Tennyson, Eliot, Sophocles, Ovid, Homer, Beckett, Joyce, Hopkins, Heaney, Anouilh … are not as easily dislodged as statues'.[134]

Significantly for you, the Snowflake Generation, these examples are not rare. Such apologist, anti-literary tosh is now a mainstream consequence of tutors' obsession over recent decades in decolonising their own curriculum, a regular feature of academic discourse in all major universities and across disciplines. If I were you, I would be far more worried about the threat these trends pose to the quality of your education than worrying who is fronting your university's PR and fund-raising campaigns.

You occupy an academy rotting from within. Worse, it often uses you, dear reader, as a stage army to purge itself of ideas – even curricula – it feels uncomfortable with. Every time these institutions have backed down or buckled under at the merest hint of a free-speech

---

134 Sarah Pett, 'It's time to take the curriculum back from dead white men', The Conversation, 8 May 2015

controversy, it's either been more about their cowardly reluctance to take on the responsibility of their own authority or because they themselves have an ambivalent attitude to their own traditional mission.

So that is how you are reflecting rather than challenging opinion, but I also want to warn you of the danger of being condescended to in the process. If you really want to be rebels, you need moral autonomy; such independence is a precondition for making history. That will mean cutting the apron strings that tie you to those adults who treat you like dependent children. It should mean rejecting patronising endorsements from the likes of Rutgers professor Brittney Cooper, who, writing in Salon, is happy to justify your actions as young adults even when she acknowledges that you often behave 'like petulant toddlers demanding to be heard'. Apparently, that is okay because 'out of the mouths of babes...' She goes on to make a virtue of your emotional incontinence and the very unreasonableness of your responses in offence disputes, especially if you are a young POC: 'Black folks have been reasoning with white people forever. Racism is unreasonable, and that means reason has limited currency in the fight against it.'[135] This assumption that you don't need reason to get what you want insults your intelligence and really is offensive. You should rebel against such condescension.

Indeed, you might be worried that a common thread in many offence controversies is the way that self-righteous older generations are often outraged on your behalf and make excuses for your thin-skinned histrionics. This does not denote respect, but is based on a view of you as childlike, vulnerable and in need of adult protection. This rather insulting brand of paternalism assumes that you are even more hapless and hopeless than any caricature of Generation Snowflake implies.

I really believe that you are better than that. And it is important because if we, as older generations, continue to pander to your hyper-sensitivity, wrap you in cotton wool and let you accept that 'small social slights … might cause searing trauma', we are setting you up for a fall. Real life will throw far more difficulties at you than

---

135 Brittney Cooper, 'It's not about you, white liberals: Why attacks on radical people of color are so misguided', Salon, 8 April 2014

unintended snubs or triggering poems. If we let you carry on being preoccupied with such microaggressions without a fight, how on earth will you be able to cope with the very real macroproblems that your generation face? If a whole generation lacks the resilience and sense of proportion to handle the vicissitudes of interpersonal interactions and everyday life, how will you confront, let alone tackle, the huge social challenges of everything from economic crises to ISIS terrorism? There is no such thing as a mollycoddled rebel. You need to toughen up.

Dear Generation Anti-Snowflakers,

I know many of you – hopefully most of you – are not wilting flowers and are as exasperated as I am by your peers when they cry at offensive emails or complain about the potential trauma of reading a racy novel. Fortunately, there has been something of a backlash lately. Good, but I fear it's not enough and frequently emanates from a minority of academics, political commentators or libertarians rather than you. Often, it is confined to pithy speech wars on social media rather than a more substantial critique. To be frank, it is you who should be more instrumental in leading the charge, and you need to be armed with philosophy, the wisdom of the ages, and a thorough-going, imaginative, future-orientated project rather than merely trading clever hashtags. So, what to do? Let's start by looking at what not to do:

Don't just be an un-PC rebel lashing out

Increasingly, people are beginning to react against the repressive PC atmosphere on and off campus by being as un-PC as possible. Abusive Twitter trolling can be an arm's-length, often anonymous way that some people vent their frustration against petty bans and 'tone policing', a means of lashing out against self-righteous social justice types demanding that everyone else shuts up, or else. It is even noticeable that laddishness seems to have grown in prevalence as the stultifying priggishness of you-can't-say/do/think-that activism has become more prominent. No doubt frat boys in the US and rugby clubs on UK campuses have always behaved boorishly. But when the LSE Rugby Club used the very public platform of the Students' Union 2015 Freshers' Fair to give out leaflets full of crude, sexist comments and featuring their offensive club rules such as a ban on 'homosexual debauchery', one suspects this was deliberate feminist-baiting.

Certainly, some of you who are becoming increasingly infuriated by the narrow, prescriptive, humourless climate of censorship choose to be gratuitously provocative – not only to wind up the easily shocked, but also to break the taboos. I have sympathy with some of your reactions against today's so called social justice warriors (SJWs), who so often exaggerate their own pain as victims, to demand they are heard while silencing and demonising any dissent. Under this provocation, the instinct to say the unsayable, even when it can lead to using vicious bile to fight vicious bile, is at least understandable. I share that feeling sometimes and want to shriek in rage and frustration when I hear the likes of those who silenced and humiliated Sir Tim Hunt unashamedly and brazenly screaming in indignation that they are the real victims.

So I get the temptation to lash out. And however

offensive you've been, I am happy to defend you of course. But, in the end, we need to do more than all become mini-me versions of Katie Hopkins.

It is more than a joking matter

In his influential article 'Rise of the Cultural Libertarians', Allum Bokhari points out that because humour can be in short supply among the easily offended, 'cultural authoritarians ... [who] take themselves too seriously or are excessively earnest' are easy to wind up. Hence, critics now regularly use the tactic of 'needling their foes with waspish critiques', concluding that 'satire [is] highly effective' as a weapon.[136]

This sort of mocking ridicule and caustic, mischievous goading can certainly be a witty way of 'skewering critics'. 'I have an idea for trolling feminists', wrote an anonymous user on the internet forum 4Chan. 'Let's see if we can get them to ban mistletoe because it "promotes rape culture".' Inevitably, thousands were fooled

---

136 Allum Bokhari, 'Rise of the Cultural Libertarians', Breitbart, 24 August 2015

and #SayNoToMistletoe was retweeted earnestly. The outraged called for a ban of the Christmas tradition of a peck under the mistletoe because it encourages men to indulge in 'nonconsensual kissing'. Within days, in a grotesque version of life imitating art, Cornell University demanded that students and staff avoid mistletoe, because it 'doesn't create an inclusive environment'.[137] Clearly funny and entertaining but, in the end, humour is a lightweight reaction to the seriousness of the problem.

Don't play them at their own game

There is a danger that these japes do little more than create a tit-for-tat, name-calling atmosphere on social media that eventually amounts to trying to play the Snowflakers at their own game. You say #YesAllWomen, I say #NotAllMen. You say feminist, I say #Meninist. Although 'meninism' is described as 'A (satirical) belief showing the hypocrisy of first-world feminism by flipping the sexes

---

137 'Feminists Claim Christmas Tradition "Promotes Rape Culture"', Breitbart, 10 December 2015

and complaining about men's rights in a similar way'
(according to the Urban Dictionary), it has evolved into
serious attempts at pushing men's identity politics. With no
hint of irony, there are demands for male-only safe spaces,
for formal recognition of International Men's Day on university campuses, and a litany of complaints centring on
how hard it is to be a man: shorter life expectancy, higher
suicide rates, negative media portrayals, and so on. This
aping of feminism's victimhood, by stressing that young
men are suffering more than their female counterparts, can
only further entrench Generation Snowflake tendencies
in our culture. In this worldview, we are all encouraged
to wallow in our vulnerability; we are all pathetic.

Clearly it can be tempting to enter the competitive
victimhood race, especially when embroiled in an argument. I repeatedly have to bite my lip when confronted
with someone who thinks that simply stating 'As a rape
victim, I find that offensive...' is an actual argument. I
want to check their privilege, to parade my own credible
scars just to win the point. But we all know, surely, that
that would be counter-productive, as it merely endorses
victimhood as an achievement and weakens the case for

arguments based on political principles, objective analysis and philosophical insights.

Don't give them a taste of their own medicine

Another version of competing with the censors on their own terms is when we try to give them a taste of their own medicine. Because so many have been hounded out of the public square by the unpleasant tactics of the easily offended, it can be seductive to try and turn the tables. But hounding 'feminazis', calling for bans on the banners, calling out 'feminist bullshit', hypocrisy-hunting through 'doxing' ('compiling and releasing a dossier of personal information on someone to discredit them') – all these tactics can be just as chilling as the sort of censorship they are intended to counter.

You may well burn with vengeance that when the intolerant persecute others, they seem to get off scot-free. But campaigns to destroy their reputations can mean shooting yourselves in the foot. Fair enough to rage against the maddening doublespeak of Goldsmiths University's Students' Union diversity officer Bahar

Mustafa when she excused her abusive '#killallwhite-men' and '#whitetrash' tweets as feminist 'in-jokes', used to reclaim 'the power from the trauma many of us experience as queers, women, people of colour, who are on the receiving end of racism, misogyny and homophobia daily'. But petitions to force her to resign, formal accusations of bullying or cheering critics who trawled her social media accounts for evidence of 'hate speech' (that led to her being arrested and charged with sending malicious communications), seem dangerously counter-productive. It endorses official policing of speech and shows a selective approach to freedom of expression, sacrificing it to achieve real justice. Sound familiar? That's Generation Snowflake's excuse. Worse, in this game of one-upmanship, we avoid having to argue. We lose any democratic sense of people conversing and arguing with each other and instead we compete to silence each other.

And while it can be infuriating when the thin-skinned elevate trivial slights to the status of historic civil rights battles, anti-Snowflakers need to be wary of aping the same tactics. It was a disgrace when protesters disrupted the guest speech by the former director of the Shin Bet, Ami Ayalon, at the King's College Israeli Society by breaking glass windows, smashing chairs and shouting 'Nazis'.[138] But comparing it to *Kristallnacht* and condemning the disrupters as 'neo-fascists' is unhelpful hyperbole aimed at playing the victim card ourselves. Smearing opponents doesn't win the argument.

Don't let's kid ourselves we are winning

Admittedly, some of your attempts at dealing with the climate of thin-skinned censoriousness are well-intentioned, often imaginative, and have admirably created a community of virtual vigilantes, such as many of those who identify around the #GamerGate hashtag, who refuse to be cowed by SJW censors. While there are dangers that this attempt at solidarity can create its own echo chamber and self-referencing identity group,

---

138 'King's College Investigates "Hate Attack" Against Israel's Ex-Secret Service Chief Ami Ayalon', Huffington Post, 21 January 2016

at least this is an attempt to be robust and positive in dealing with an often fatalistic mood of demoralisation in the face of endless bans. Liberal commentator Nick Cohen summed up the despair that many in my generation feel about how young radicals seem to have been seduced by the 'delusion that you can censor your way to a better tomorrow', when he wrote: 'Fighting it can feel almost impossible.' Cohen describes how many good people have been driven out of left-wing politics because 'some pointy-nosed prig accuses them of siding with the enemy because they did not realise that words which were acceptable yesterday are unacceptable today'.[139]

So it is cheering that many of you optimistically believe that 'younger movements' of resistance, such as 'cultural libertarianism', are gaining traction. But while these initiatives certainly have inspiring, formidable and – dare I say – older heroines (such as American writers Christina Hoff Sommers, Cathy Young,

---

139 Nick Cohen, 'The PC revolution devours its own', Writing from London blog, 28 March 2015

Camille Paglia and, in the UK, Maryam Namazie, Julie Bindel and Joanna Williams), I am less convinced by Allum Bokhari's argument that the offence industry is a 'small segment of the population' and 'increasingly unpopular with the public'. I don't buy his assurance that sympathy for the pernicious forms of 'progressivism and feminism' that have done so much harm to free speech is 'rapidly evaporating in academia, on the web, in arts and entertainment … on the mainstream Left'. These trends are too deeply entrenched to be uprooted by a backlash against their most egregious form. Bokhari concludes: 'To fight them … all you have to do is ignore them – or, better yet, mock them.' If only it were that easy. But I fear that if you focus entirely on the pantomime villains of progressives, feminists, online SJWs and the most flagrant irrationalities of offence politics, you may underestimate and be distracted from taking on the broader cultural problems of the 'vulnerable' individual and the climate of fear that has softened up so many of your peers, making them ripe to finding words and ideas so frightening and hurtful.

A new model of personhood, a new philosophy of freedom

I think your task needs to be more far-reaching and ambitious and requires nothing less than beginning to carve a new cultural model of personhood.

Christopher Lasch in his analysis of narcissistic culture notes that 'every society reproduces its culture – its norms, its underlying assumptions, its modes of organising experience – in the individual, in the form of personality'. Today's *zeitgeist* is the pathologised individual. You are living in an era where the 'form of personality' that is valued and privileged is the vulnerable victim, where weakness is treated sympathetically and strength is demonised as arrogance or bullying, where anything smacking of the stiff upper lip is seen as a relic from a cruel, insensitive era. Today, emotional literacy is *de rigueur*.

So, to make real gains, you need to create new cultural norms, a new personality type, to take on the deeply ingrained safety-first culture that has so crippled your peers. You may be tempted to think that all you need to do then is to just tell the Snowflakers that they need to develop a backbone. Yes, it would be worth explaining that we are all offended at times, but that need not mean acquiescing to censorship; that if we grow a thicker skin, we will be robust enough to argue back, to shrug off hurt feelings, even hateful insults. In this context, proselytising traditional virtues such as stoicism, fortitude and strength of character would be a positive step forward. But as we are not nineteenth-century Victorians, you will need to articulate a modern version of what might constitute the best version of human beings that we can imagine.

For starters, instead of the contemporary miserablism that always sees the worst in human motives and activities, with its mean-spirited, misanthropic nihilism, I would urge you to cultivate a philosophical outlook that emphasises a sense of human potential, and looks to every individual's strengths rather than assuming their weaknesses, their creativity rather than their destructiveness. Most crucially, you will need to frame a generational aspiration for the future that replaces safety as the end goal. You will need to wage war against all those trends discussed in Part II that suggest that anything that keeps people secure and comfortably risk-free should trump all other considerations, from civil liberties to free speech. What is more, a key task will be to develop your own philosophy of freedom, no less, one that disentangles (and saves the credibility of) radicalism and progressive fights for equality and justice; one that rescues freedom of thought from the toxic imposition of acceptable orthodoxies; one that forges a vibrant sense of autonomy.

How do you that? Well, it's your fight, so you will need to find your own way, but you could do worse than to stand on the shoulders of giants. Perhaps start with those modern radical philosophers who struggled with the existential questions of their time about how we should deal with our human condition of being 'condemned to be free'. What would Sartre say about safe spaces? How would Camus react to #RhodesMustFall? What would Simone de Beauvoir think about identity politics?

You will need to be brave and face down those who want to shut you up: say what you believe, as though the easily offended were not there to silence you. Thumbs up to those LSE students who have just set up a 'speakeasy' to counter the safe space movement on campus; Inevitably, other LSE students immediately tried to no-platform the society but it's a great initiative and encouraging that it looks to be spreading nationally.[140] And I can only commend Warwick University undergraduate George Lawlor's personal crusade against the insulting 'I Heart Consent Training Sessions'. He realised he would be denounced as 'a bigot, a misogynist, a rape apologist' because he dared to declare that he didn't 'have to be taught to not be a rapist. That much comes naturally to me, as I am sure it does to the overwhelming majority of people you and I know.'[141]

Hear, hear. We need more such rebels. You could do worse than trying it for yourself in your own sphere of influence. But to avoid being isolated as George

---

140 'LSE students: We don't want to live in a university safe-space bubble', *Evening Standard*, 24 January 2016

141 George Lawlor, 'Why I don't need consent lessons', *The Tab*, 14 October 2015

was, you need to build a proper movement that can demonstrate its solidarity with everyone who faces censorship. That even includes defending those SJWs' right to argue reactionary, anti-free speech positions. You need a solidarity that uniformly upholds free speech for all, whether it is so-called 'feminazis' such as Bahar Mustafa, crude comics like Dapper Laughs, censoriously PC comedians like Kate Smurthwaite, or anyone who holds idiotic views you despise (as well as those you sympathise with).

It is essential to ensure that our universal values are not fractured by a form of sectarian ghettoisation. So, you will need to be a beacon of Enlightenment values that fights for hearts and minds. This might mean defending the right to be offensive for those Western Islamists who endorse ISIS as an example of your consistent commitment to freedom, while simultaneously arguing uncompromisingly against their anti-freedom barbarism. You must be confident enough to separate principles and errant practices.

To you all...

I end with a call to arms for you all, because I can't give up on the Snowflakes just yet: you're young, you have time to change. You all need to toughen up and make a virtue of the right to be offensive. It's an easy sentence, but actually it's a challenge: take hold of your destiny and sort out this mess. Whether you are Snowflakes or anti-Snowflakers, you need to learn the trick of turning subjective outrage into measured, passionate, coherent argument capable of convincing others, rather than retreating into your respective self-erected camps, whether safe-space bubbles or free-speech echo chambers. You have a chance to shape the future as you want it, independent of and in defiance of the contemporary mood of fear and loathing. History is yours for the making. It's an exhilarating challenge, an exciting adventure, a necessary task. And if it's any use, do call on those of us who have not retreated into adult colouring books, who won't pander to you in a patronising or infantilising way, who credit you with more gumption than to think you need our protection. There's still a substantial minority of people in the older generations who believe in free speech – no ifs, no buts – and we are a resource you should turn to. But, ultimately, this is your generation's fight. Good luck.